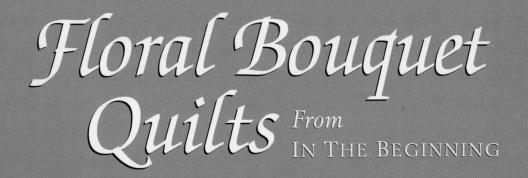

Floral Bouquet Quilts From In The Beginning

Sharon Evans Yenter

Welcome to My Garden

As a toddler in Minnesota, I loved my father's garden of colorful flowers and beautiful climbing vines. Shortly after the photo on the previous page was taken, our family piled into my grandparents' 1941 Ford sedan and headed for the great Pacific Northwest, the land of opportunity. We settled in Seattle, Washington, my dream city then and forever.

My father continued to grow fragrant roses, sweet peas, gladiolus, nasturtium, hollyhocks, and pansies. With moisture and sunshine, the flowers grew in bountiful profusion.

My first entrepreneurial adventure was at the age of five selling pansies door-to-door in our tightly knit neighborhood. The pansies were inserted in small mounds of brown clay—my selling point being that you didn't need a vase to display them! All of our neighbors seemed delighted with my floral artistry and the pennies and nickels grew in my small muddy hands.

If this was a job, I was hooked! Unfortunately, my mother closed my flower business before the formerly abundant garden was bare, but not before my lifelong love of retail had taken root.

When my children were young, I sewed patchwork items for boutiques and craft fairs, standing in the wind and rain with my colorful quilted products blowing around me. One day, between cloudbursts, I dreamed of opening a real store with a roof, where quilters could come for classes, inspiration, and friendship. I imagined a better way to spread the word of the wonders of quiltmaking and here it is—after twenty-three years of careful attention, it's in full bloom: In The Beginning Fabrics—my glorious flower garden!

Trish Carey (L) and Sharon enjoying an exuberant discussion at the In The Beginning fabric retail store in Seattle.

Dedication

To all quilt shop owners, teachers, authors, and staff members who spread the word and have kept the legacy of quiltmaking alive and strong, going into the 21st century. And in memory of Nancyann Johanson Twelker (1933-2000), quiltmaker, teacher, historian, author, and friend.

Foreword

I recently attended a large marvelous quilt show in Seattle sponsored by the Association of Pacific Northwest Quilters. The entries were from Oregon, Washington, Idaho, Montana, Alaska, Alberta, and British Columbia, Canada. The design and workmanship were superb.

As I worked in the In The Beginning booth at the Merchant Mall, I enjoyed seeing longtime friends and customers. I noticed many of us are not going gray; we're getting blonder and blonder. Fifty- and sixty-year-olds are not what they used to be!

I came of age in a generation where I had to raise my skirt and show my legs to get a "stewardess" job, weigh in before a flight, agree to remain unmarried, and quit my job at age thirty-two because "male passengers like to have young attractive women serving them"!

My retail management-training program wasn't much better. It was explained that I would never be more than a buyer because women were not promoted beyond that level and "besides, men make better bosses." I was not allowed to buy a house, have a credit history, or apply for a credit card in my name, even though my salary was equal to many men. The comment was always, "You might get pregnant, have to quit your job and then who would pay"?

In 1964 all of that changed and discrimination against women was outlawed with passage of the Civil Rights Act. In the late '60s and early '70s, women were able to make demands with legislation to back them up. The Equal Credit Bill was passed in the early '70s and banks were barred from discriminating on the basis of race, creed, or sex.

The bi-centennial of 1976 made a deep impression on me and I came to appreciate the beauty, creativity, satisfaction, and history of quiltmaking. In 1977, I opened my quilt shop, In The Beginning, because I could! Doors were opened to female entrepreneurs and we went on through.

The early quiltmakers, strong women who had no rights and very few choices, intrigued me— women who expressed their dreams, talents, and frustrations in their quilts. In the restrictive 1800s, bright, creative, colorful quilts were stitched, a lasting tribute to these women who are joined with us in time.

We are so fortunate to have this extraordinary heritage. Let us cherish it and pass on the tradition in the 21st century for generations to come.

I think that one's art is grown inside one.

I do not think one can explain growth.

It is silent and subtle.

One does not keep digging up a plant

to see how it grows.

—EMILY CARR

table of Contents

History 10

The early 1800s was a time of discovery with new techniques and designs in American textiles. Never-before-seen prints and colors delighted sewers.

Fabric Choice 13

Large floral bouquets, tone-on-tones, and small light prints are all you need to create glorious quilts reminiscent of the 19th century.

Color 16

Study color usage with an easy-to-understand color chart. Suggested colorations for floral quilts make your job simple.

Floral Bouquet Fabrics 20

Make the fabric "work" for you. Learn ways of working with large floral fabrics to stitch the quilt of your dreams.

Quilt Plans 22

Basic Quiltmaking Techniques 114

Clear instructions and color illustrations for making a quilt from start to finish.

a little History

I started collecting quilts over twenty-five years ago mostly because I've always sewn and loved fabrics. Those little bits of color pieced together in nostalgic patterns charmed me. Little did I dream when I made my first purchase that quilts would become my passion and lifelong career. I discovered a "Pied Piper," leading me down a magic road where I would find history and kinship with women of the past and become a caretaker of their treasures.

Our quilts are our continuity with the past, and some of the few tangible remainders of an existence on this earth, so I take my collecting seriously. My "hobby" began to resemble detective work. Who was the person who made the quilt? How and where did she/he live? Unfortunately, many quilters stitched in anonymity, yet with many of my quilts, I feel I know their nameless maker. I might have used the same colors with a particular pattern and created with the same spontaneity. Born in the same century, we would have been friends!

Hexagon Garden. One of my favorite quilts in our collection (shown at far right) was purchased in London in the late 1980s. Perhaps, because of my British Isles' heritage and the serendipitous (definition: *discovering desirable things unexpectedly*) find in a small decorator shop, I began to study quilts of the 1800-1850s era.

It was exciting to see the spacious florals used randomly and in large chunks. This quilt is a banquet of early dress and interior-furnishing fabrics. Originally called a "medallion" or "central medallion" pattern in the United States, this type of quilt, in England, would be classified as a "Frame Patchwork Quilt" by the British Quilters' Guild. It is one example of a style that accounted for approximately fifteen percent of the pieced quilts studied in a recent British Quilt Heritage Project, which documented over 3,900 British quilted items in a three-year time span. Notice this quilt has six frames around a center of hexagons, and then progresses from small cotton prints to larger-scale fabrics in the solid borders and outer triangular-pieced border. In each corner is a valuable piece of block-printed chintz, possibly imported from India.

Hexagon Mosaic. The English frame-patchwork quilt, shown below, is from a later time, probably 1830-1850. It features four frames around a center of hexagons and includes many interesting fabrics, although it does not contain

Hexagon Mosaic, Great Britain, *1830-1850, 85"x 100" (Collection of author.)*

Hexagon Garden
ORIGIN: Great Britain   DATE: 1800-1830
FINISHED SIZE: 90" x 108"   COLLECTION OF AUTHOR

the color excitement of the previous piece. I would love to see a floral bouquet fabric featured in some of the solid rectangles. (They're actually small-scale prints but read as solids.) Isn't the pink and blue with the yellow-and-white stripe terrific? It could have been made yesterday!

Simple Star, United States, 1820-1850, 70" x 70" (Collection of author.)

Simple Star. This is my Smithsonian reject. Supposedly its companion is in their collection, but this quilt was declined—my good fortune! This simple star quilt is an example of the use of patterned chintz fabric for lattices. This was an economical use of expensive fabric and shows it at its best. American cotton manufacturers had difficulty competing with French and British textile imports until the 1830s. The word "chintzy," meaning cheap, was coined reportedly because every scrap of chintz fabric was used or saved in a miserly fashion, rather than shared with others as were most cottons. Pieces of chintz might be found in the family sewing basket fifty years later. (This hoarding of precious chintz scraps is another reason it is difficult to date early quilts with certainty.)

Montpelier. Notice the pieced lattices in this quilt, entitled "Montpelier." Many chintz pieces were leftovers from clothing or extras from

Montpelier, United States, 1820-1850, 90" x 90" (Collection of author.)

home-furnishing projects, and this top includes five different chintz fabrics in the lattices. The turned-down corner shows a stunning chintz floral stripe that covers the entire back of the quilt. Rows and rows of glorious flowers impress with a fabric that was obviously purchased for the quilt, making it a "best quilt" in the household. Many of these coverings survive because they were rarely used, and were spread over the bed only when company was expected. This quilt is very large because it would have had to fit over the bulky bedding equipment, including pillows, comforters, other quilts, and bedclothes. In addition, it probably had to cover a trundle bed that pulled out at night from its daytime storage under the larger bed.

Sunflower, United States, 1840-1870, 70" x 80" (Collection of author.)

Sunflower. This is an example of a chintz fabric printed in floral strips—allowing the maker to cut the pieces lengthwise to make the quilt's borders. It is obvious that this quilt was well planned and fabric was purchased specifically for the project.

Although this is a later quilt (1840-1870), chintz was still more expensive than calico and the borders—while cut lengthwise—are pieced.

'Tis the heaven of flowers you see there;
All the wild-flowers of the forest,
All the lilies of the prairie,
When on earth they fade and perish,
Blossom in that heaven above us.
— HENRY WADSWORTH LONGFELLOW

Fabric Choice

My purpose with this book is to tempt you—if only temporarily—away from creating traditional quilts inspired by those dated from approximately 1850 to 1910, with their small-scale, grayed calicoes and predominance of browns, blacks, and rust madders. I would like to introduce you to the glorious, elegant, floral pieced quilts of a previous era—approximately 1790 to 1850. Beautiful English, French, and eventually American chintzes and medium florals were used to create sophisticated quilts in colors that were sometimes bright and at other times colonial shades of celadon, mulberry, and buttery yellow. Large and medium floral bouquets and vines danced with abandon across a neutral ground. Small prints were more curvy than later in the century, and generally lighter in color. The quilts included in this book are not meant to be exact reproductions of the earlier quilts, but are our interpretations of those masterpieces for our new century.

The secret to creating the pretty, luxurious look of early English, French, and American quilts is in fabric choice. Many of the original masterpieces were basically scrap quilts; you probably will have many suitable small-scale "go-withs" in your stash. An important difference between the quilts in this book and the quilts of the late 1800s is the size of the designs in the fabrics. Fabrics from the early part of the 19th century included small, medium, and large designs. All of these sizes were used in one quilt because fabric was

An elegant floral bouquet fabric.

scarce and most was imported. The quilts of the second half of the century, however, consisted of mostly small calico and shirting prints because the U.S. specialized in manufacturing millions of yards of small calicos at affordable prices for inexpensive clothing. Many women could afford to purchase cloth for a complete quilt and these tiny prints were all the rage. Colors were much darker and did not include the pretty soft pastels of the earlier era. Let's examine the fabrics that are essential to the success of our floral bouquet quilts. Because the pattern scale ranged from large and medium to small prints, it is important to combine them to achieve a successful floral quilt.

Chintz

Toile de Jouy

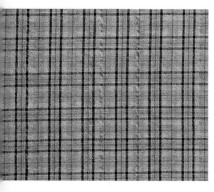

Plaids

Stripes

Chintz

Chintz is a cotton fabric that usually contains large to medium florals. It was referred to as "furnishing weight" in the 1700s to 1800s and we know it as "home decorating" material. It is recognizable by its glazed finish and heavier weight than apparel fabrics. The word chintz originated from the Hindi "chint" which means a vari-colored cloth. In the early 1600s, ships laden with spices arrived regularly in England. It is thought that some hand-painted cotton panels from India were included as gifts for company directors. Nothing of this sort had ever been seen and there was immediate interest. Up to this time, men and women had dressed in natural colored woven woolens and linens. Printed fabric had never been available. Although people loved the idea of printed material, the native Indian designs were too unfamiliar, bright, and large for the English taste.

By 1650, English and French sketches were sent to Indian artists and the chintzes were adapted to European tastes. Chintz became the fabric of choice for all those who could afford it. It was eventually printed in Europe, especially in England, France, and Holland, and became affordable and popular with the middle classes. Because of wars, trade prohibitions, and cost, chintz became very precious in the United States and was difficult to obtain. By 1830, chintz was produced in the states, but it was very expensive and European chintz was easier to obtain until the mid-nineteenth century.

Scraps of chintz in geometric shapes and lengths for borders made the best use of this fine fabric and were usually reserved for "best quilts" The popularity of machine piecing and quilting in our era has made decorator chintz a practical choice for quilts. It mixes easily with regular-weight cottons and comes in a wonderful range of color and designs.

Floral bouquet fabrics, similar to chintz florals, are suitable for our quilts and are also available in a lighter-weight material. Choose floral designs with leafy areas and tendrils to add a graceful look to your quilt.

Toile de Jouy

Pronounced *twahl duh zhwee*— the name means "fabric of Jouy (zhwee)"— this style of copperplate fabric printing originated in Ireland, and was then produced in England. It reached its glory when the printing technique was refined about 1770 by Christophe-Phillipe Oberkampf at his factory in Jouy, France. Historic events from centuries earlier as well as patriotic scenes depicting American heroes, including George Washington, were popular with American buyers. Scenes from the French countryside, including bucolic layouts that told a story, were popular worldwide. In America, both French and English toiles were used extensively in wealthy colonial homes. Although the Jouy factory closed after the death of Oberkampf in 1815, reproductions of the designs are still being produced.

These fabrics are unique for quilt backgrounds, small pieces, or lattices, and add a delicate look to any quilt.

Plaids

Plaids have been around for centuries, ever since weavers discovered they could create interesting patterns by coloring yarns before weaving them. Plaids can be printed on cotton, but most are woven by machine in the United States.

Handloomed fabrics are still available and are produced mainly in India. Small pieces of plaid are very effective with large florals and toiles.

Stripes

Stripes have been popular for several centuries and range from simple two-color designs to intricate patterns of stripes and flowers. Many were produced in France in the late 1700s through the mid-1800s and, created in chintz and brocade, were popular with the French court. Copies of floral stripes from the 1800s are available to quilters in cotton fabrics and are important to create the look of the early quilts.

Miscellaneous Prints

Small-scale cotton prints were very popular in the early nineteenth century as they were used in clothing for the working classes. It is written that the Oberkampf factory alone had over 10,000 different block-printed designs. Many of the designs consisted of floral "sprig" motifs on a pastel ground. Roses were popular and were included in many miniature designs. The use of tone-on-tone florals, eclectic elements, trailing ribbons, cherubs, urns, and picotage were common.

Picotage

In France, Christophe-Phillipe Oberkampf introduced the picotage effect by using metal pins to make small dots on the fabric surface. He interspersed these among florals and tonal patterns to create a shaded design. Look for various different beige tones and soft grayed pastels with flowers and picotage in a number of these prints in reproduction fabrics available today. Many of these prints in soft colors and similar values are important for the quilts in this book.

Paisleys

The curvy, intricate scrollwork designs that we have come to know as Paisley were originated in India during the 1600s, but did not arrive in France until the early 1800s. Legend has it that Napoleon Bonaparte bought exquisite shawls for Josephine in India and she became the envy of the French court. The cost of a shawl was the price of a small house, so there was much prestige attached to it. This fashion accessory quickly became popular with French and English upper classes in the early 1800s. A small town in England called Paisley became a major supplier of woven shawls that were made available worldwide by the year 1850. Manufacturers block printed these designs for garments and home furnishings, and Paisley-style designs became an important fabric motif throughout the 1800s. These patterns work especially well in quilts as they lend a soft, graceful, multi-colored accent.

Rose Prints

Stylized Floral Prints

Picotage

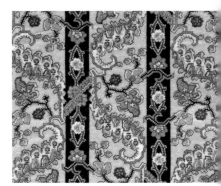

Paisleys

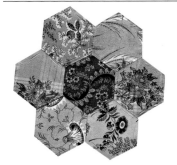

This hexagon block, which we in the U.S. call a "Grandmother's Flower Garden," originated in England. Historically it is the most popular quilt pattern in that country and was referred to as "Honeycomb." This block was found in the city of Bath in Great Britain and is dated 1825 from the papers basted inside the fabric hexagons.

With color, for the price of a pot of paint, people can express their own style and individuality. But, as with style, a gift for color has to be developed by experiment. If you don't dare, you are doomed to dullness.

— SHIRLEY CONRAN

Color

Subdued, relaxed, romantic, sweet, dramatic, tranquil, sublime, charming, warm, nostalgic, exhilarating, magical, elegant, vibrant, fresh.

Aren't these wonderful words? They all create a mood that can be conveyed by color. Perhaps it is because I live in an area with a gray climate that I am so sensitive to color. I enjoy watching the bursts of red, bright blue and teal cars, orange taxis, yellow delivery trucks, and lime green and purple billboards as they wash across the rainy-gray palette of my studio window.

I believe many quilters are super sensitive to color; their shelves of beautifully hued cloth are like medicine for the soul. Our spirit needs the nourishment of glorious color.

The study of color can be very complicated and intense with theories and hypotheses that quickly make our eyes glaze over. There are many disciplines a fine artist working with oils, watercolors, or dyes needs to know that a quilter can easily skip over. There are also many fine books devoted entirely to color listed in the Resources section on page 124.

For the purposes of this book, I'll give you basic advice about color, which I have tried to simplify. This information should be sufficient for about ninety percent of your quilts. If you have the special intuitive sense of color that many quilters have, do not limit yourself by the rules. Although if you analyze certain color combinations, you may find that your instinct is so perfect it has been following the rules all along!

Here's one of my favorite formulas for choosing colors for a quilt:

- Pick a floral fabric with many screens of color. For example, the "Garden Twist Bouquet" fabric shown at right has thirteen screens. Each screen is a color, so there are that number of colors to choose from when selecting a palette for a quilt, plus tints, tones, or shades of each hue. Pull several colors from the bouquet. Use differing amounts as accents. The amounts in your quilt should be unequal. Remember you may use black, white, gray, or beige with any of the colors. I prefer to use "off white" rather than a harsh, pure white. Off white is often called "decorator white."

- Many fabric companies present coordinating groups of fabric that are very grayed down in shades or tones that are quite dull. The results are flat, uninteresting quilts. Always remember to use a color a couple of degrees lighter and brighter from another collection of fabric to add sparkle to a quilt, or a couple of shades darker but more intense to add drama. Also mix warm and cool colors for interest. Golds and reds do wonders for dark quilts!

■ Remember, you can use shades, tints, and tones of a color, not just the hue, found on most color wheels. On the following pages I have flattened the color wheel, which might give you an easier reference for choosing your fabrics. Study the tints, hues, tones, and shades in the charts. Find materials in your stash to match some of the squares. Refer to the larger color wheel on page 18 and then practice composing color schemes using the diagrams on page 19.

It's obvious that this chart is a very limited representation of the millions (yes, millions!) of colors in existence.

An interesting pastime is visiting a paint or home-supply store and studying their paint displays. The mixtures and relationships of hues are fascinating. Choose color chips for a quilt and see if you can match them to fabric in your local quilt shop. Don't feel guilty about taking the color strips. You'll probably want to paint an accent wall in a room later to highlight your quilt.

A floral bouquet with the chips of the color screens used to print the fabric.

Color Charts

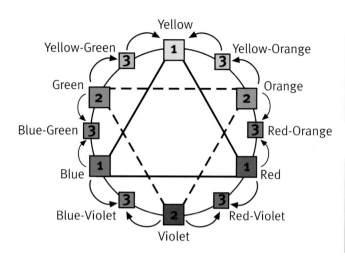

Cool Colors

SHADE	TONE	HUE	TINT

3 Yellow-Green

2 Green

3 Blue-Green

1 Blue

3 Blue-Violet

2 Violet

The numbers on the color wheel correspond with the numbers of the hues on the chart and the definitions below.

1 **Primary Colors:** yellow, red, blue

2 **Secondary Colors:** orange, violet (purple), green; created by mixing parts of 2 primary colors.

3 **Intermediate Colors:** yellow-orange, red-orange, red-violet, blue-violet, blue-green, and yellow-green; created by mixing equal parts of a primary and its closest secondary color.

Hue: the name of the purest form of a color

Tint: mixing the hue with white

Tone: mixing the hue with gray or with its complement

Shade: mixing the hue with black

Chroma: degree of brightness or intensity of a color

Value: the relative lightness or darkness of a color

A tint is considered a light value, while a shade is a dark value. Color groupings of the same value would be shades of different hues, tones, or tints used together.

Warm Colors

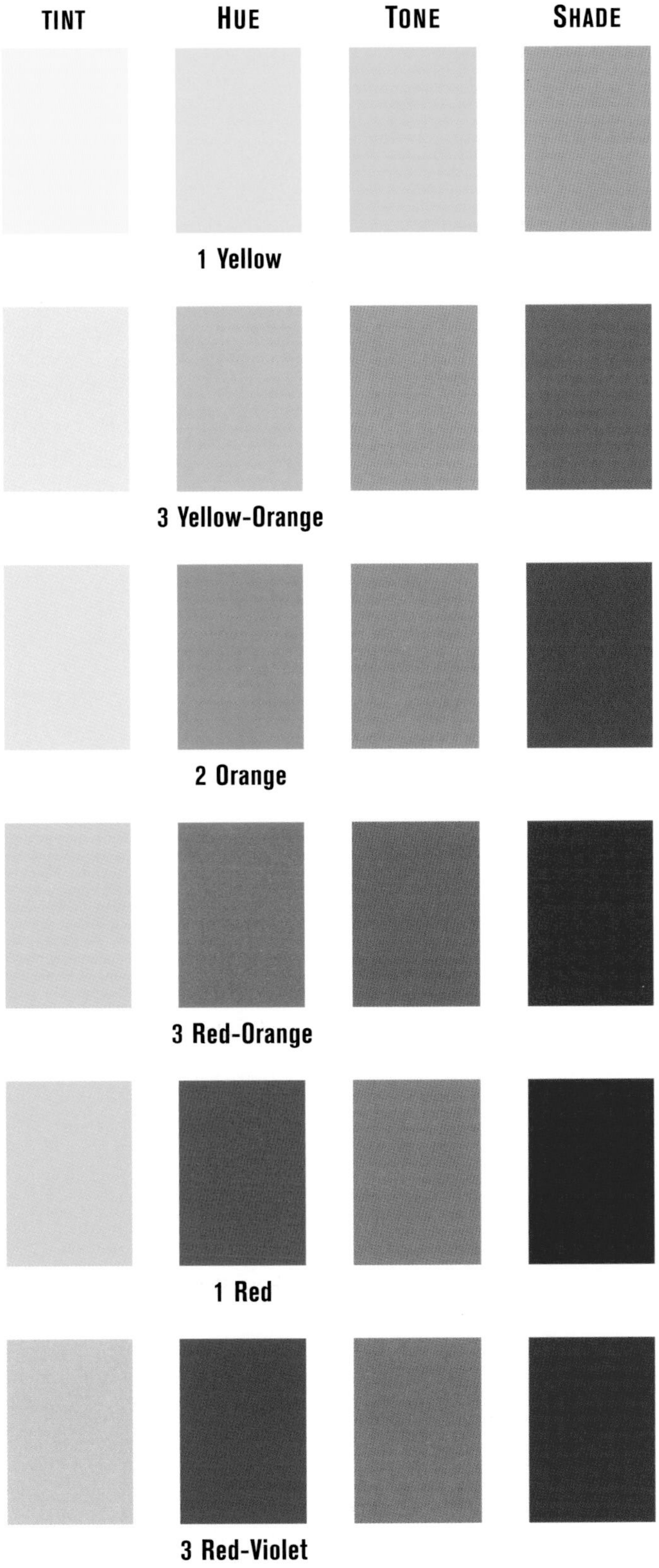

TINT
HUE
TONE
SHADE
1 Yellow
3 Yellow-Orange
2 Orange
3 Red-Orange
1 Red
3 Red-Violet

Color Schemes

Complementary:
Two colors opposite each other on the color wheel

Yellow
1
2
Violet

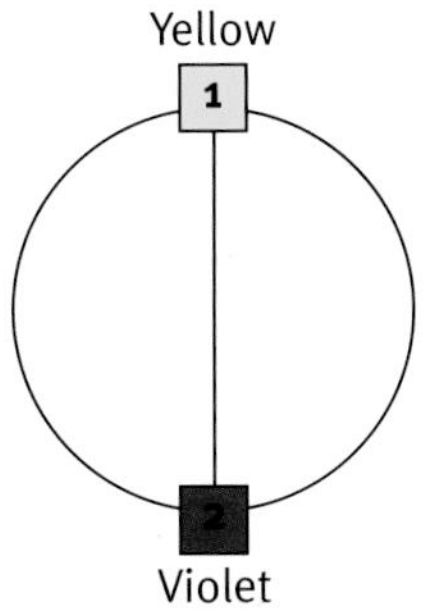

Triadic:
Any three colors equidistant from each other on the color wheel

Yellow
1
Blue
1
1
Red

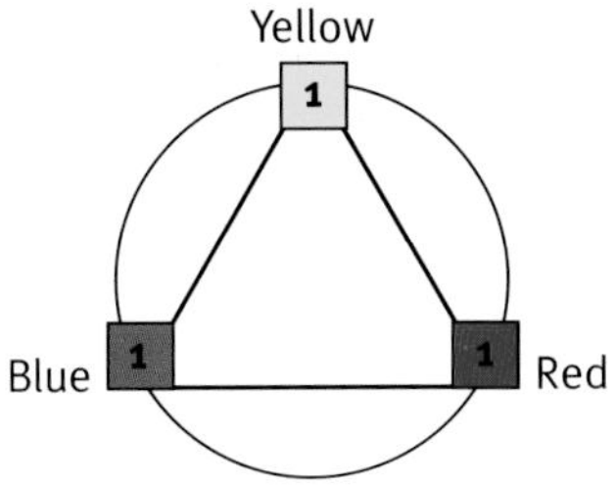

Analogous:
Any two or three adjoining colors on the color wheel

Blue-Green
3
Blue
1
Blue-Violet
3

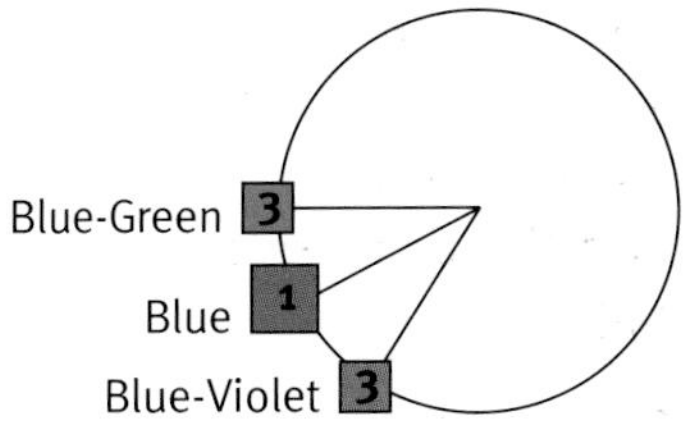

Split Complementary:
The two colors on each side of a color's complement

Yellow-Green
3
Blue-Green
3
1
Red

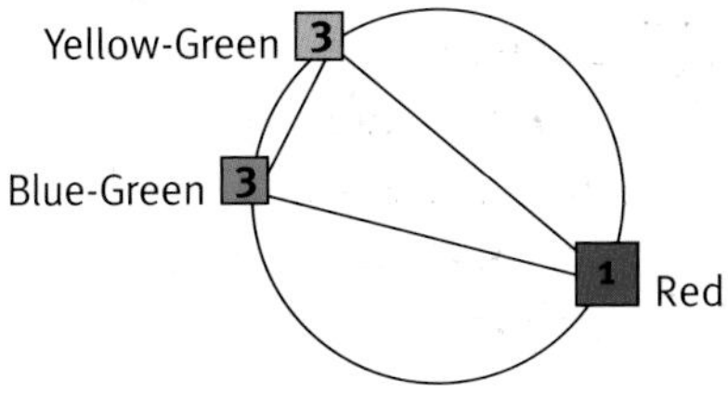

Double Complementary:
Any two adjoining colors on the color wheel plus their complements

Yellow
1
3
Yellow-Orange
Blue-Violet
3
1
Violet

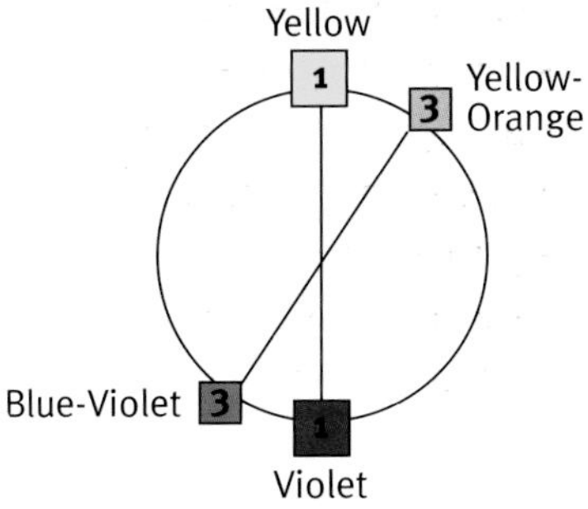

Monochromatic:
A group of hues, tints, or shades of a single color

Achromatic:
A group of blacks, whites, and grays

We'll talk of sunshine and of song,
And summer days when we were young;
Sweet childish days that were as long
As twenty days are now.

— WILLIAM WORDSWORTH

working with Floral Bouquet *fabrics*

In this book, quick techniques and simplified patterns allow the floral bouquet fabrics to do much of the work. Large florals eliminate the necessity of intricate piecing and make your job easier.

There are two main color techniques used in the quilts in this book. The first technique contains definite light, medium, and dark values to make the patchwork designs work. Use as much contrast as you want to make your quilt as soft or as vibrant as you like.

Oceans of Flowers

Quilts based on this technique include Oceans of Flowers *(shown above)*, Chinese Chain *(p. 22)*, Seattle Stars *(p. 108)*, Sawtooth Star *(p. 96)*, Log Cabin Garden *(p. 78)*, Chintz Squared *(p. 84)*, Garden Swirl *(p. 52)*, English Checkerboard *(p. 28)*, Le Jardin *(p. 64)*, and Strippy Floral *(p. 40)*.

There are many techniques you can use for choosing a contrasting color scheme.
- You may use the easy formula explained in the color section, where you extract colors from the floral bouquet. Fabric designers follow color rules so your combinations have already been chosen correctly.
- Study the color schemes shown on pages 18 and 19 and use the color wheel to create your own color grouping. You might try an analogous or triadic scheme using light, medium, and dark components of each color.

The remaining quilts in the book feature a low-contrast technique, which means that all the fabrics should be a similar value, but not necessarily the same value. Value determines where a color is positioned on a scale of light

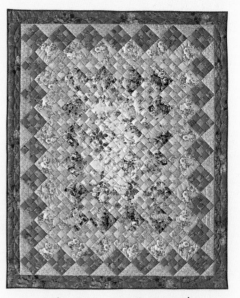

Gingersnap Ninepatch

to dark. Most of the fabrics in these quilts are of medium-high to high value, with white being the highest value. The colors go from beige to white grounds and contain softly colored motifs. For example, if a rose floral motif in a patch is peach colored, you may repeat that hue as a background print for another patch. Work at your design wall and play with your choices. Stand back and squint your eyes. The fabrics should blur together and create a lush surface. None should stand out unless you purposely choose this as a design element. Study the center of Gingersnap Ninepatch (shown at left) for an example of this technique with bits of contrast added for interest.

Cutting Considerations

Many of the quilts in this book were designed to include one or more large floral bouquet fabrics, reminiscent of decorator chintzes but now available in lighter-weight cotton for quilters. There are some things to consider when cutting the pieces for your quilts.

Blocks: When you cut strips from floral bouquet fabrics, you may want to cut them randomly, or decide to selectively place the ruler to include certain amounts of the bouquets. Many of the quilts use only portions of a bouquet to get the softness of flowing leaves and tendrils. You may decide to use more dense floral bouquets for the center blocks of your quilt.

If you want dense flowers completely filling every block, make a see-through cutting template from template plastic, the size of your block, including seam allowance. Cover the floral bouquet fabric with the template and move it around until you find a design you like. Trace a line around the template with permanent pen or pencil, and cut out the fabric with scissors.

Position template for selective cutting.

If you want a scrappier look to your blocks, cut strips and then crosscut pieces from the strips. You can use most of the pieces that include flowers, leaves, and tendrils, discarding solid background pieces.

Borders: If you want a particular portion of the bouquet to show up regularly and evenly in all four borders, you will need to plan the border carefully. Many of our quilts are planned with uneven bouquet borders, but we pay attention to the corners of the quilt. It is important that a bouquet meets another bouquet, or at least a partial bouquet, at the inner corners. This creates a graceful, floral curve around the quilt.

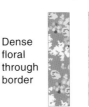
Dense floral through border

Dense portion of floral at inner edge of borders

Yardage Considerations

Your cutting decisions as well as the floral design can affect yardage requirements. For the quilts in this book, yardage requirements for the floral bouquet fabrics are generous. In most cases, the borders are cut from the length of the fabric, rather than from the width, to avoid piecing seams that would create distracting breaks in the floral pattern.

Study the pattern you are following, and the floral bouquet fabric you want to use, to decide just how you want to cut it. If your plan varies from the way the quilt in the photo was done, you may need extra yardage.

I usually cut my borders nine to twelve inches longer than needed so I can work with the fabric to decide how I want the bouquets to meet in the corners. I often skip the dense centers of the bouquets so the borders are more open.

Selective cutting may yield odd pieces of background areas. You can often use them for smaller pieces in the quilt or to make coordinating pillows, adding a finished touch to a room.

Border   Border

Scrap   Scrap   Scrap

Chinese Chain

A SMALL TEA SHOP IN OUR AREA DISPLAYS A SIGN THAT SAYS:

1 teapot, you're a tea drinker
2 teapots, you're a real tea drinker
3 teapots, you're a collector!

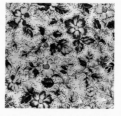

I love blue and white porcelain and have collected antique Chinese, Japanese, and English teapots for years. It's been a long, exciting process and I now have a nice collection. I guess I'm not a "more is better" kind of person, but a "better is better" individual. I may only get one piece every year or two, or even three, but it gives me the opportunity to read and become knowledgeable about my collection. ❧ It's always good to have an inexpensive collection too. It allows friends, children, or family members a chance to find a "special" gift for a holiday or birthday. ❧ A tip: Try to choose your own collectible items. A friend dislikes frogs, so a co-worker brought her a frog figurine as a joke. She received several more from well-intentioned friends who thought they liked them, and a collection was born. Now as she opens her frog gifts, she smiles and raves to be polite. She loves the joy "selecting the perfect frog" brings to her children and admits the "little critters" are growing on her.

A pretty blue monochromatic bouquet creates serenity in a room.

Chinese Chain

Two simple, traditional blocks link together to create the chained effect
in this easy quilt. With only strips and squares to cut for the blocks,
this one's easy enough for a beginner.

DESIGNED BY: **Sharon Yenter** QUILTED BY: **Sherry Rogers**
FINISHED SIZE: **60" x 68½"** FINISHED BLOCK SIZE: **6" x 6"**

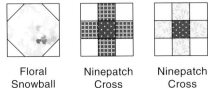

Floral Snowball Block A Ninepatch Cross Block B Ninepatch Cross Block C

Directions for "Basic Quiltmaking Techniques" begin on page 114.

Cutting Instructions

Cut strips across the width of the fabric from selvage to selvage, unless otherwise directed.

Floral Bouquet
- 4 strips, each 6½" wide; crosscut 20 squares, each 6½" x 6½"

White
- 13 strips, each 2½" wide; crosscut 80 squares, each 2½" x 2½"; set remaining 8 strips aside for strip units

Dark blue print
- 4 strips, each 2½" wide

Medium blue prints (4)
- 2 strips, each 2½" wide, of each print

Yellow prints (4)
- 2 strips, each 2½" wide, of each print

Yellow print
- 5 strips, each 1¼" wide, for inner border

Blue print
- 2 strips, each 9¾" wide; crosscut 5 squares, each 9¾" x 9¾"; cut each one twice diagonally for 18 (2 extra) side setting triangles
- From the remaining strip, cut 2 squares, each 5⅛" x 5⅛"; cut each square once diagonally for 4 corner setting triangles
- 6 strips, each 2" wide; set aside for middle borders

Blue and white floral print
- 4 strips, each 6¾" wide, *along the length of the fabric;* set aside for outer borders
- 4 strips, each 2½" wide, set aside for binding

Block and Border Construction

Block A: Floral Snowball
All seam allowances are ¼" wide.
1. On the wrong side of 80 white 2½" squares, draw a diagonal line from corner to corner with a pencil.

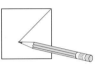

2. With right sides together, place a white square in each corner of a 6½" floral square, taking care to orient the lines as shown. Stitch on each line, then trim away the excess at each corner, leaving ¼"-wide seam allowances. Press the seams toward the corner triangles.

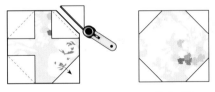

Make 20.

3. Repeat with the remaining floral bouquet squares to make a total of 20 Floral Snowball blocks.

Blocks B and C: Ninepatch Cross
1. Cut each 2½"-wide dark blue, medium blue, and yellow strip in half crosswise. Cut each of 8 of the 2½"-wide white strips in half crosswise.

Chinese Chain

Fabric Requirements
44"-wide fabric

- Blue-and-White Floral Bouquet for Snowball blocks - 1 yd.
- White for background - 1⅛ yds.
- Dark blue print for Ninepatch blocks - ⅜ yd.
- 4 Medium blue prints for Ninepatch blocks - ¼ yd. of each
- 4 Yellow prints for Ninepatch blocks - ¼ yd. of each
- Yellow print for inner border - ¼ yd.
- Blue print for setting triangles and middle border - 1 yd.
- Blue and white "all-over" floral print for outer border and binding - 2½ yds.
- Backing - 3⅞ yds.
- Batting - 64" x 73" piece

2. Using half-strips of dark blue and each medium blue print, make 4 Strip Units A. Cut 4 segments, each 2½" wide, from each strip unit for a total of 16.

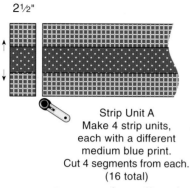

2½"

Strip Unit A
Make 4 strip units,
each with a different
medium blue print.
Cut 4 segments from each.
(16 total)

3. Repeat step 2, using the yellow half-strips and the remaining dark blue half-strips to make 4 Strip Units B. Cut 4 segments, each 2½" wide, from each strip unit for a total of 16.

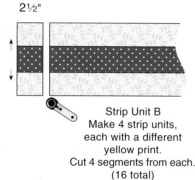

2½"

Strip Unit B
Make 4 strip units,
each with a different
yellow print.
Cut 4 segments from each.
(16 total)

4. Using white half-strips and the remaining medium blue and yellow half-strips, make Strip Units C and D. Cut 8 segments from each unit for a total of 32 of three-patch Unit C and 32 of Unit D.

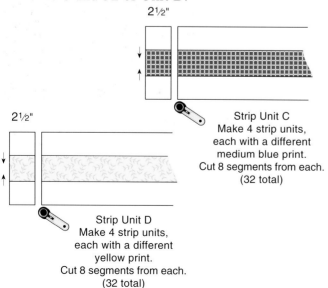

2½"

Strip Unit C
Make 4 strip units,
each with a different
medium blue print.
Cut 8 segments from each.
(32 total)

2½"

Strip Unit D
Make 4 strip units,
each with a different
yellow print.
Cut 8 segments from each.
(32 total)

5. Arrange and sew the three-patch units into Ninepatch Cross blocks, making sure to use matching fabrics for each block. Press seams in one direction. Make a total of 30 blocks. (You will have a few three-patch segments left over to put in your scrap box.)

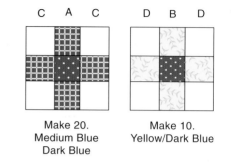

C A C   D B D

Make 20.
Medium Blue
Dark Blue

Make 10.
Yellow/Dark Blue

Quilt Top Assembly

1. Following the diagram for placement, arrange the blocks in an alternating fashion, beginning and ending each row with Ninepatch Cross blocks. Add a blue side setting triangle to each end of each row of blocks. Sew the blocks and triangles together in diagonal rows. Press the seam allowances toward the Floral Snowball blocks in each row, and toward the setting triangles at the end of each row.

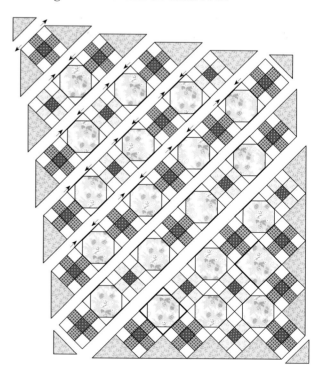

2. Sew the rows together and press the seams in one direction.

3. Add a corner setting triangle to each corner of the quilt top and press the seams toward the triangles.

Borders

1. Sew the 5 yellow inner border strips together to make one long strip. Press seams open. Repeat with the 6 blue middle border strips.

2. Measure the length of the quilt top through the center and cut two inner border strips to match this measurement. Sew one border strip to each side edge of the quilt top. Press the seams toward the borders.

3. Measure across the quilt top from side to side, including the borders you just added. Cut two inner border strips to match and sew the borders to the top and bottom edges of the quilt top. Press the seams toward the borders.

4. Measure for, cut, and add blue middle borders to the quilt top as you did for the inner borders. Press the seams toward the yellow inner border.

5. To add the floral outer borders, measure for and trim the 6¾"-wide floral border strips as you did for the previous borders. Sew to the quilt top and press the seams toward the floral borders.

Finishing

1. Layer the quilt with batting and backing.

2. Baste the quilt layers together. Mark and quilt as desired.

3. Trim the excess batting and backing even with the quilt top edges.

4. Sew the binding strips together to create one long strip. Bind the quilt edges.

5. Add a hanging sleeve if desired. Sign and date your finished quilt.

Home Decorating Hints

⌒ Always group each small-sized collection together for impact.

⌒ Make a wall quilt to display with your collection.

English Checkerboard

O WNING MY STORE HAS OPENED MANY DOORS TO TRAVEL FOR me and I've had the opportunity to visit wonderful places and meet terrific people. ❧ In 1989, I won a trip to England compliments of a wholesale trade publication. This was a random drawing and says much about my good luck. I've always subscribed to the theory that the "harder you work, the luckier you get," so this was an un-expected treat for me. ❧ One of the highlights of my visit was a shopping trip at the Liberty of London store in midtown London. It's a large store, housed in an older build-ing reminiscent of a department store of the early 1900s—all dark wood and balconies. It's a treasure trove of oriental rugs, gift items, clothing, a lovely tea room, and—best of all—their wonderful fabric. ❧ My son Jason was studying in London at the time, and I had arranged to meet him in the evening. As I was happily sorting through stacks of fabrics, I felt some-one looking at me. I glanced up to see Jason and a friend standing nearby. "We were on our way to a matinee, but I knew I would find you here, so we came in," he said. A city of mil-lions and he knew where to find me! ❧ We fabric lovers are all the same. We'll never get lost. If a fabric shop exists in a town, we'll show up eventually. Just don't find us too soon!

Large floral bouquets give this quilt a lovely English cottage appearance.

English Checkerboard

The beloved Irish Chain pattern takes on the look of a lovely flower garden in
this fresh variation. A profusion of flowers is scattered in the well-planned
garden, complete with checkerboard paths between the plots.

DESIGNED BY: **Sharon Yenter**   QUILTED BY: **Margy Duncan**

FINISHED SIZE: **60" x 80"**   FINISHED BLOCK SIZE: **10" x 10"**

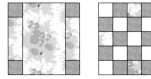

Floral Bouquet
Irish Chain

Checkerboard

Directions for "Basic Quiltmaking Techniques" begin on page 114.

Cutting the Floral Bouquet Fabric Pieces

Important: Cut the floral bouquet pieces in the order given.

1. Cut 7 strips, each 2½" wide, across the width of the fabric. Set aside for Units 1 and 3 in the Checkerboard block.
2. From template plastic, cut a 6½" x 10½" rectangle and a 2½" x 6½" rectangle.
3. Center the large template over the densest part of the floral bouquet print and select the area you wish to cut for each of 18 Floral Bouquet blocks. Trace around each one with pencil or removable marking pen. Cut out the rectangles with rotary cutter and ruler or shears. The flowers in each piece need not be exactly the same in each rectangle, but should densely fill the space. Check the size of each cut rectangle and square up as necessary so that each one measures 6½" x 10½". Use rotary cutting equipment for accuracy.

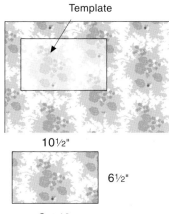

Template

10½"

6½"

Cut 18.

4. Use the smaller template to mark and cut 36 rectangles as described in step 3. Select areas to cut with a densely patterned area next to less dense background area to create the look of the edge of the bouquet. Square up as needed.

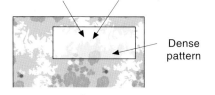

Template plastic   Less dense pattern

Dense
pattern

Cut 36.

Cutting Instructions

Cut all strips across the width of the fabric from selvage to selvage.

Green tone-on-tone (dark chain)
- 5 strips, each 2½" wide; crosscut 72 squares, each 2½" x 2½", for Floral Bouquet Irish Chain blocks
- 19 strips, each 2½" wide; set aside for Checkerboard blocks

Light background print
- 14 strips, each 2½" wide; set aside for Checkerboard blocks

Pink-and-white print
- 8 strips, each 1½" wide, for inner border

Green tone-on-tone print
- 8 strips, each 4½" wide, for outer border

Binding
- 8 strips, each 2½" wide

English Checkerboard

Fabric Requirements
44"-wide fabrics

Choose a dense floral bouquet fabric for the center of the Floral Bouquet blocks.

- Floral Bouquet fabric - 3½ yds.
- Green tone-on-tone for dark chain - 1⅞ yds.
- Light background, small print for light chain - 1¼ yds.
- Pink-and-white print for inner border - ½ yd.*
- Green tone-on-tone for outer border - 1⅜ yds.* *Borders are pieced. Allow for more fabric if you prefer to cut borders in one piece.
- Binding - ⅝ yd.
- Backing - 5 yds.
- Batting - 64" x 84" piece
- Template Plastic - 11" x 14" piece

Floral Bouquet Irish Chain Block Assembly

All seam allowances are ¼". Follow pressing directions carefully, taking care not to stretch the completed units.

1. Sew a 2½" green (dark chain) square to opposite ends of each 2½" x 6½" floral bouquet rectangle. Press the seams toward the squares.

Make 36.

2. Sew two floral/green strips from step 1 to opposite sides of each 6½" x 10½" floral bouquet rectangle with densest part of pattern next to the large rectangle. Press seams toward the strips.

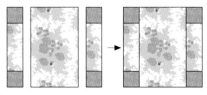

Make 18.

Checkerboard Block Assembly

1. Sew 2½"-wide strips together in the order shown below. Press all seams toward the darker fabric in each unit. Crosscut the required number of 2½" segments from each unit.

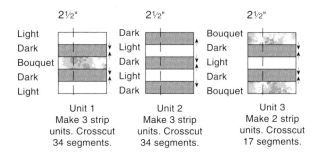

2½"	2½"	2½"
Light	Dark	Bouquet
Dark	Light	Dark
Bouquet	Dark	Light
Dark	Light	Dark
Light	Dark	Bouquet
Unit 1	Unit 2	Unit 3
Make 3 strip units. Crosscut 34 segments.	Make 3 strip units. Crosscut 34 segments.	Make 2 strip units. Crosscut 17 segments.

2. Following the diagram below, arrange the segments to make 17 Checkerboard blocks. Sew segments together for each block and press seams toward the center in each block.

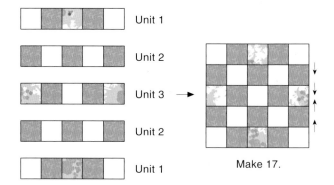

Unit 1
Unit 2
Unit 3
Unit 2
Unit 1

Make 17.

Quilt Top Assembly

1. Following the quilt layout, arrange and sew the Floral Bouquet Irish Chain and Checkerboard blocks in horizontal rows. Press the seams toward the Floral blocks in each row.

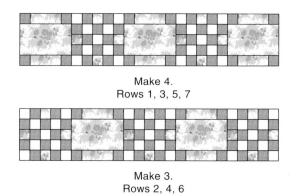

Make 4.
Rows 1, 3, 5, 7

Make 3.
Rows 2, 4, 6

2. Arrange the rows in numerical order and sew together, matching seams carefully. Press the seams in one direction.

Borders

1. Sew the inner border strips together in pairs, using diagonal seams. Press the seams open.
2. Measure the quilt top length through the center and cut 2 inner border strips to this measurement. Sew to the long edges of the quilt top. Press the seams toward the borders.
3. Measure the quilt top width through the center, including the border you just added, and cut 2 border strips to this measurement. Sew to the top and bottom edges of the quilt top. Press the seams toward the borders.
4. Repeat steps 1-3 for the outer borders and press the seams toward the outer borders.

Finishing

1. Layer the quilt top, batting, and backing. Baste the layers together.
2. Mark and quilt as desired or quilt diagonally through the center rows of the squares, and outline quilt selectively around floral bouquets for added depth. Quilt the border in a design of your choice.

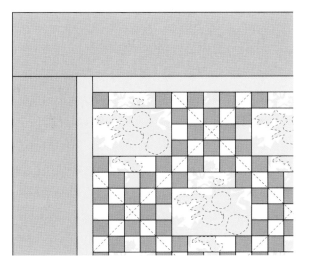

3. Trim the batting and backing even with the quilt top edges.
4. Sew the binding strips together to make one long piece. Bind the edges of the quilt.
5. Add a hanging sleeve if desired. Sign and date your finished quilt.

Home Decorating Hints

⌐ Use an armoire to display your quilts. It's a great way to protect them and it's fun to open the doors when entertaining.

⌐ Line the back of the armoire with fabric from your stash. Pushpin it in place or back selvages with double-faced tape.

Gingersnap Ninepatch

EVERY AUTUMN WE FLY TO HOUSTON, TEXAS TO SELL OUR NEW fabric lines to shop owners attending International Quilt Market, a gigantic wholesale show. Because In The Beginning is a small, growing company, we have not seen the need to buy the huge closet-sized crates most companies bring to the show—so we pack everything for our booth in suitcases!  There are six of us attending who have the luxury of one suitcase each plus twelve suitcases for the show. Last Market we appeared at the baggage area, lugged our bags from the carousel, counted them—yes, eighteen here—and headed outside to get a rental van and taxi. Everything went well until the next day as we were setting up our booth, when we discovered one suitcase was missing—the large bag that contained most of our quilts including the lovely Ninepatch pictured here. My son, Jason, spent much of the day conversing with helpful airport personnel but to no avail. They searched everywhere and found nothing. It had been a day and a half since first missing the suitcase and the personnel held out little hope. Later that night an airport police officer called to report he had found our suitcase on the curb! Was it taken by mistake or stolen and returned? We'll never know, but we think it was the "Quilter Angels" in town for the big quilt show!

Mix a higher contrast floral to make the flowers jump out of the quilt.

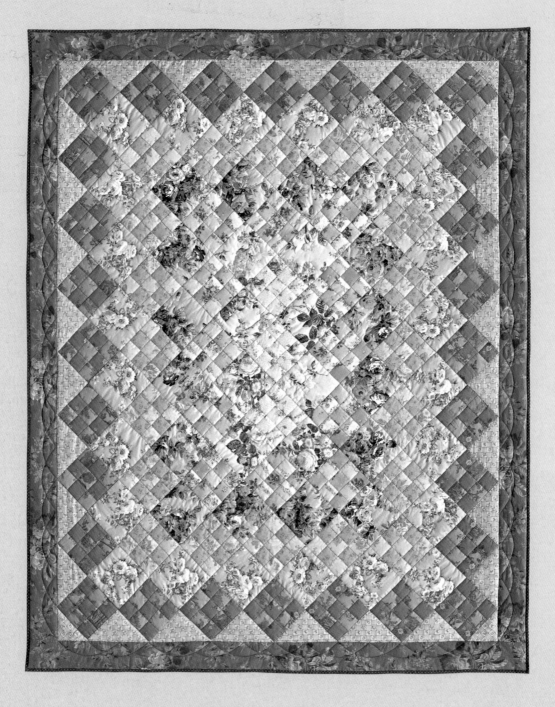

Gingersnap Ninepatch

Pink and green floral squares and tone-on-tone Ninepatch blocks surround a light center to make this softly shimmering quilt. Wouldn't it be perfect one cool, crisp morning to wrap up in it and settle in a cozy corner with a cup of tea, croissant, and a romantic novel?

DESIGNED AND QUILTED BY: **Margy Duncan**

FINISHED SIZE: **65" x 85"**   FINISHED BLOCK SIZE: **6" x 6"**

Floral Onepatch

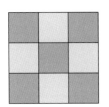

Ninepatch

Directions for "Basic Quiltmaking Techniques" begin on page 114.

Cutting Instructions

Cut all strips across the width of the fabric from selvage to selvage.

Floral Bouquet #1 (grayed off-white)
- 2 strips, each 6½" wide; crosscut 8 squares, each 6½" x 6½", for Floral block A

Floral Bouquet #2 (pink)
- 3 strips, each 6½" wide; crosscut 16 squares, each 6½" x 6½", for Floral block B

Floral Bouquet #3 (green)
- 4 strips, each 6½" wide; crosscut 24 squares, each 6½" x 6½", for Floral block C

Grayed off-white print #1 Ninepatch A
- 3 strips, each 2½" wide

Grayed off-white print #2 Ninepatch A
- 3 strips, each 2½" wide

Pink print #1/Ninepatch B
- 5 strips, each 2½" wide

Pink print #2/Ninepatch B
- 4 strips, each 2½" wide

Pink print #3/Ninepatch C
- 8 strips, each 2½" wide

Pale green print/Ninepatch C
- 7 strips, each 2½" wide

Light fern-green print/Ninepatch D
- 8 strips, each 2½" wide

Dark fern-green print/Ninepatch D
- 10 strips, each 2½" wide

Print for Setting Triangles
- 2 strips, each 9¾" wide; crosscut 7 squares, each 9¾" x 9¾"; cut twice diagonally for a total of 28 side setting triangles
- 1 strip, 5⅛" wide; crosscut 2 squares, each 5⅛" x 5⅛"; cut once diagonally for four corner setting triangles

Floral print for Border
- 9 strips, each 4½" wide

Binding
- 9 strips, each 2½" wide

Gingersnap Ninepatch

Fabric Requirements
44"-wide fabrics

- Floral Bouquet #1 (grayed off-white background) - ½ yd.
- Floral Bouquet #2 (peachy pink background) - ¾ yd.
- Floral Bouquet #3 (soft green background) - 1 yd.
- Grayed off-white print #1 for Ninepatch A - ¼ yd.
- Grayed off-white print #2 for Ninepatch A - ¼ yd.
- Pink print #1 for Ninepatch B - ½ yd.
- Pink print #2 for Ninepatch B - ⅜ yd.
- Pink print #3 for Ninepatch C - ¾ yd.
- Pale green print for Ninepatch C - ⅝ yd.
- Light fern-green print for Ninepatch D - ¾ yd.
- Dark fern-green print for Ninepatch D - ⅞ yd.
- Coordinating print for setting triangles - ⅞ yd.
- Border (large floral on dark fern-green background) - 1½ yds.
- Binding - ¾ yd.
- Backing - 5½ yds.
- Batting - 69" x 89" piece

Ninepatch Block Assembly

1. Make the required number of strip units for each set of Ninepatch blocks as shown in the diagram. Press seams in the direction of the arrows.

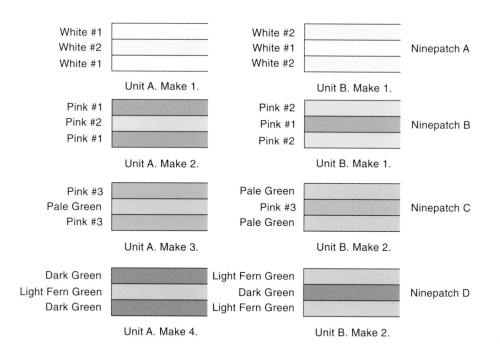

White #1
White #2
White #1

Unit A. Make 1.

White #2
White #1
White #2

Ninepatch A

Unit B. Make 1.

Pink #1
Pink #2
Pink #1

Unit A. Make 2.

Pink #2
Pink #1
Pink #2

Ninepatch B

Unit B. Make 1.

Pink #3
Pale Green
Pink #3

Unit A. Make 3.

Pale Green
Pink #3
Pale Green

Ninepatch C

Unit B. Make 2.

Dark Green
Light Fern Green
Dark Green

Unit A. Make 4.

Light Fern Green
Dark Green
Light Fern Green

Ninepatch D

Unit B. Make 2.

2. Cut the required number of 2½" segments from each of the strip units as indicated in the diagram.

3. Arrange the segments and sew together to make the required number of each Ninepatch block. Press seams in one direction.

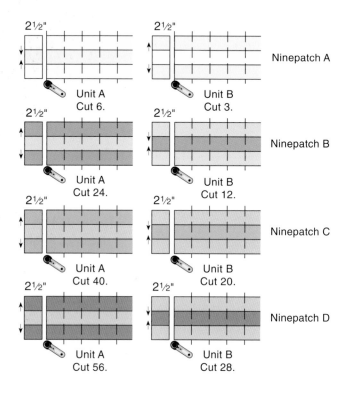

2½"

Ninepatch A

Unit A
Cut 6.

2½"

Unit B
Cut 3.

2½"

Ninepatch B

Unit A
Cut 24.

2½"

Unit B
Cut 12.

2½"

Ninepatch C

Unit A
Cut 40.

2½"

Unit B
Cut 20.

2½"

Ninepatch D

Unit A
Cut 56.

2½"

Unit B
Cut 28.

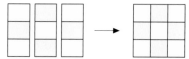

Make 3.
Ninepatch A

Make 12.
Ninepatch B

Make 20.
Ninepatch C

Make 28.
Ninepatch D

Quilt Top Assembly

1. Following the quilt layout and, paying careful attention to color placement, arrange the blocks and side setting triangles in diagonal rows. Sew together in rows. Press the seams toward the Floral Onepatch blocks in each row, and toward the setting triangles at the end of each row.

Row 1 Row 2 Row 3 Row 4 Row 5 Row 6 Row 7
Row 8 Row 9 Row 10 Row 11 Row 12 Row 13 Row 14 Row 15

2. Add a small setting triangle to each corner of the quilt top. Press the seams toward the triangles.

Borders

1. Sew the 4½"-wide green floral border strips together end to end in pairs, using diagonal seams. Press the seams open.
2. Measure the quilt top length through the center and cut 2 border strips to this measurement. Sew to the long edges of the quilt top. Press the seams toward the borders.
3. Measure the quilt top width through the center, including the border strips you just added, and cut border strips to this measurement. Sew to the top and bottom edges of the quilt top. Press the seams toward the borders.

Finishing

1. Cut the backing fabric into two equal lengths and sew long edges together. Press seam open.
2. Layer the quilt top, batting, and backing. Baste the layers together.
3. Mark and quilt as desired.
4. Trim the batting and backing even with the quilt top edges.
5. Sew the binding strips together to make one long piece. Bind the edges of the quilt.
6. Add a hanging sleeve if desired. Sign and date your finished quilt.

Home Decorating Hints

— Scatter photos of "instant relatives" around the room. Most antique stores have old photos that need to be rescued. Adopt them and create a mood. Write "Not a relative of _____" so future generations are not in fear of their children getting the big ears and odd nose of faux "Uncle Harry."

— Place your bed at a diagonal and hang a curtain to create extra room for storage behind it. You do not need a four-poster bed as photographed here; hooks and a curtain rod will do.

Strippy Floral

EARTBROKEN—I LOVE THE LITTLE FRAMED PICTURE IN this photo. It's a postcard from the early 1900s with a pensive, young woman and the word "Heartbroken" printed underneath. The most sentimental thing about the card is the writing in pencil that says, "Do you ever get this way?" One hundred years ago girls had their hearts broken as badly as they do today. ∾ I get impatient when I see the phrase, "a kinder, gentler, easier time" in women's magazines today. Unless you were wealthy, you didn't have a jovial maid as in the movies and life was not all strolling, singing, and tea parties. You cooked, cleaned, grew and canned many of your foods, and sewed most of the family's clothes. ∾ My grandmother, Mary O'Connor, was a dressmaker in the early 1900s and worked mostly full time sewing special garments for the women in her small town. She also managed to raise four children in her spare time. ∾ A dressmaker was a luxury for the average woman in the late 1800s through the turn of the century. Because many women could afford only one good dress, it had to do for marriage, special occasions, funerals and even their own burial. Many were married in black. These women had the same sadness, dreams, and joys as we do. Their lives were challenging—then as now—just different. ∾ On a happier note, let's subscribe to the glorious 1940s musicals' notion of what life was like in earlier times. Create a romantic, soft bedroom hideaway. You'll feel as if you're in a Technicolor MGM movie!

Fabrics selected convey

a feeling of a lush,

summer garden.

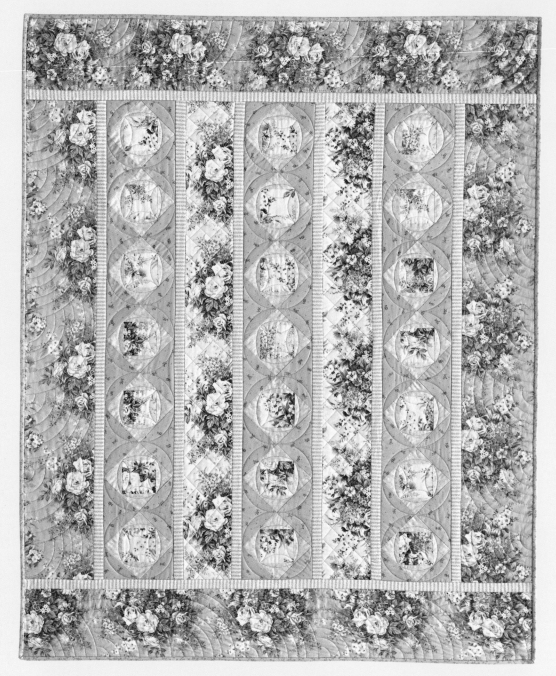

Strippy Floral

Muted striped pathways lead you through neatly arranged flower plots in this strippy floral quilt. Pieced blocks alternate with strips of a light floral bouquet; border strips of its twin print—in refreshing sage green—wrap around the garden, resembling a wall of climbing roses.

DESIGNED BY: **Sharon Yenter**   QUILTED BY: **Sherry Rogers**

FINISHED SIZE: **55⅞" x 66⅞"**   FINISHED BLOCK SIZE: **5" x 5"**

Square-in-a-square
Finished size: 5"

Directions for "Basic Quiltmaking Techniques" begin on page 114.

Cutting Instructions

Cut strips across the width of the fabric from selvage to selvage, unless otherwise directed. Cut floral bouquet strips along the lengthwise grain to avoid piecing seams.

Peach tone-on-tone

- 4 strips, each 3⅜" wide; crosscut 42 squares, each 3⅜" x 3⅜"; cut once diagonally for a total of 84 triangles for the blocks

Sage sprigged print

- 2 strips, each 8⅜" wide; crosscut 9 squares, each 8⅜" x 8⅜"; cut twice diagonally for a total of 36 side setting triangles for the pieced strips
- 1 strip, 4¼" wide; crosscut 6 squares, each 4¼" x 4¼"; cut once diagonally for a total of 12 corner triangles

Sage/white stripe

- 8 strips, each 1½" wide, for sashing between pieced and floral strips

Peach/white stripe

- 3 strips, each 1½" wide, for sashing between pieced and floral strips

White background floral

- 2 lengthwise strips, each 5½" x 54",* for interior strips
- 2 lengthwise strips, each 4" x 54", crosscut 21 squares, each 4" x 4", for the block centers

Sage background floral

- 2 lengthwise strips, each 8" x 50",* for outer borders
- 2 lengthwise strips, each 8" x 54",* for outer borders
- * These whole-cloth strips are all a little longer than necessary; you will trim them to match the length of the pieced strips later.

Block Construction

1. Sew a peach triangle to opposite sides of a 4" floral square. Press the seams toward the triangles. Add triangles to the remaining two edges and press. Repeat with the remaining 20 floral squares to make a total of 21 blocks.

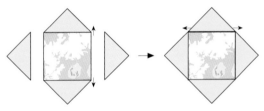

Make 21.

2. Sew the short side of two sage side setting triangles to opposite sides of 15 floral squares. Press the seams toward the side setting triangles.

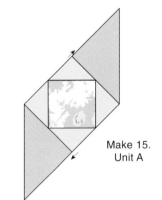

Make 15.
Unit A

Strippy Floral

Fabric Requirements
44"-wide fabric

- White background Floral Bouquet for strips and blocks - 1¾ yds.
- Sage background Floral Bouquet for outer borders - 1¾ yds.
- Peach tone-on-tone - ½ yd.
- Sage sprigged print for setting triangles - ⅞ yd.
- Sage/white stripes for sashing - ½ yd.
- Peach/white stripes for sashing - ¼ yd.
- Sage tone-on-tone for backing and binding - 3½ yds.
- Batting - 60" x 70" piece

3. Sew a triangle to one edge of each of the 6 remaining floral squares.

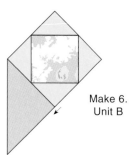

Make 6.
Unit B

4. Arrange the squares and sage corner triangles to make 3 rows of 7 blocks each. Sew the diagonal rows together, adding corner triangles last. Press all seams toward the sage triangles. It will be necessary to "twist" the seam at the block point intersection in each seam to do so.

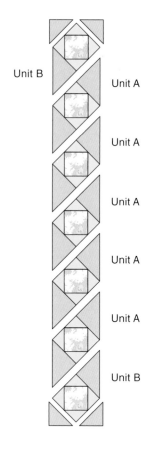

Unit B

Unit A

Unit A

Unit A

Unit A

Unit A

Unit B

Quilt Top Assembly

1. Measure the length of the pieced strips, taking care not to stretch them. If all three do not measure the same, take an average of the three measurements. You will need to piece 3 sage/white striped sashing strips to match this measurement. Take care to match the stripe carefully to avoid a visual break in the stripe pattern.

2. Trim the 50"-long border strips of the sage floral bouquet to match the length of the striped sashing strips.

3. Arrange the pieced squares, striped sashing strips, and border strips and sew the strips together. Press all seams away from the strips of pieced squares. One seam will be pressed toward the sashing strip and the other toward the adjacent floral strip.

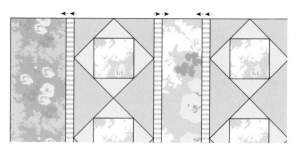

4. Measure the quilt top width at the center and each end, and average the measurements if not the same.

5. Piece 2 peach/white striped strips to match the measurement from step 4, and trim the 2 remaining sage floral bouquet border strips to match. Sew a striped sashing strip to one edge of each border strip. Press the seam toward the border.

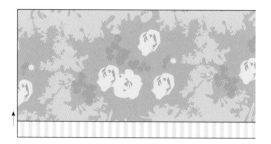

Finishing

1. Cut the backing fabric into two 1¾-yard lengths and sew together. Trim to 60" x 70" for the backing.
2. Cut 2⅜"-wide strips from the remaining fabric and sew together to make 7½ yards of binding.
3. Layer the quilt with batting and backing.
4. Baste the quilt layers together. Mark and quilt as desired or follow the suggestion below.

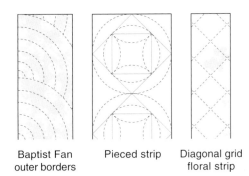

Baptist Fan outer borders   Pieced strip   Diagonal grid floral strip

5. Trim the excess batting and backing even with the quilt top edges.
6. Sew the binding strips together to create one long strip. Bind the quilt edges.
7. Add a hanging sleeve if desired. Sign and date your finished quilt.

Home Decorating Hints

⌐ Drape filmy, inexpensive wedding tulle behind the bed. Some is very wide (120") so ask for it.

⌐ Buy small lace pieces at garage sales — dresser scarves, hand towels, and tablecloths. Soak in Biz® then wash as usual to remove stains.

⌐ Find a worn-looking iron bed and an old chandelier. You don't have to wire this, just hang it from a large plant hook. If you are patient and willing to "shop" awhile, you can find these items inexpensively.

Lottie's Pride

M Y HUSBAND PURCHASED AN ANTIQUE DOUBLE NINEPATCH QUILT from a dealer several years ago as a special gift for me. There was no information with the quilt as to maker or place of origin. It was another of the thousands of quilts existing that were created by anonymous quilt-makers. ❧ While studying the fabric and small details of the quilt, I found barely visible, awkward embroidery that spelled, "Horse Fell On Me Yesterday. Mar 7 1894." Did a horse really fall on her or was this an expression of illness or despair? My friend, Ann Stohl, who grew up in South Dakota says her mother used to say she "fell down a hay hole" when feeling out of sorts. ❧ Was her quilt all that this anonymous quiltmaker had to confide in? I hear her over one hundred years later and wish I could have comforted her. This is the wonder and delight of quiltmaking—a connection with women through time. ❧ I remade the quilt in elegant French 1800s reproduction fabric. I named the quiltmaker Lottie because there is also an "L" embroidered on the original quilt. The young woman in the picture frame is someone's lost and lonely relative. I thought she and the quilt went well together and named her Lottie.

Gracious toiles and widely spaced florals mix beautifully.

Lottie's Pride

With so many gorgeous floral fabrics available, it is difficult to limit the fabrics to just a few in each quilt. This scrappy quilt offers opportunities for using many different florals, either purchased as fat quarters or other small quantities. Mix low contrast fabrics that blend and then add darker or lighter colors so some squares jump out.

DESIGNED BY: **Sharon Yenter**   QUILTED BY: **Sherry Rogers**
FINISHED SIZE: **63½" x 63½"**   FINISHED BLOCK SIZE: **9" x 9"**

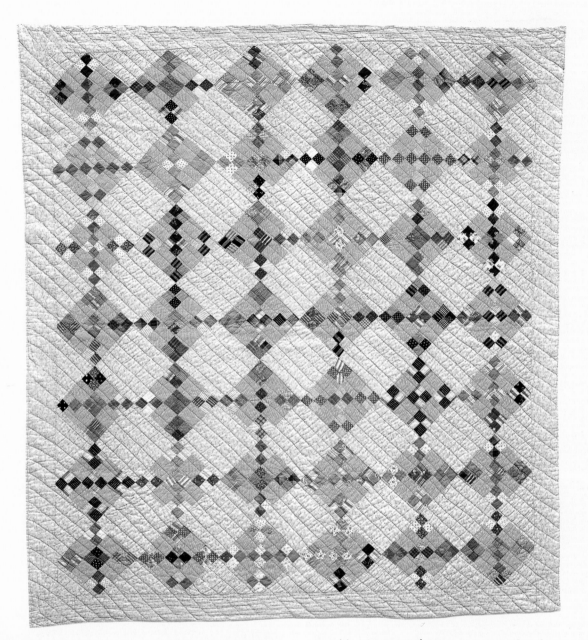

Double Ninepatch, Anonymous quiltmaker, 1894, (Collection of author.)

A close-up of embroidered area of the quilt with the initials L.B. and the phrase "Horse Fell On Me Yesterday. Mar 7, 1894."

This is the original double ninepatch quilt from the 1890s. The ninepatch was a common traditional pattern because the design was effective using scraps. The alternate blocks and borders of the quilt probably contain a fabric which was purchased for this project. Notice the small calicoes and shirtings which are typical of the period. Nothing was wasted. Clothing was recycled and, for variety, scraps were traded with friends and neighbors.

Lottie's Pride

Fabric Requirements
44"-wide fabrics

- Note: Fat quarters are 18" x 22" pieces.
- Light background Floral Bouquet for setting squares - 1 yd.
- Light and medium prints for setting triangles - 4 fat quarters
- Medium or dark prints for Double Ninepatch blocks (Fabrics A, B, and C) - 3 fat quarters
- Light print for Double Ninepatch blocks (Fabric D) - 1 fat quarter
- Assorted light, medium, and dark prints for Double Ninepatch blocks - 12 or more fat quarters
- Dark Background (green) Floral Bouquet for outer border - 2½ yds.
- Green print for binding - ⅝ yd.
- Backing - 4 yds.
- Batting - 68" x 68" piece

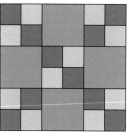

Double Ninepatch

Directions for "Basic Quiltmaking Techniques" begin on page 114.

Cutting Instructions

Light Floral Bouquet
- 3 strips, each 9½" wide, cut across the fabric width; crosscut 9 squares, each 9½" x 9½", for the setting squares

Light and Medium prints
- From each of 3 fat quarters, cut 1 square, 14" x 14"; cut each square twice diagonally for a total of 12 side setting triangles
- From one of the fat quarters, cut two squares, each 7¼" x 7¼"; cut once diagonally for 4 corner setting triangles

Medium and Dark prints (Fabrics A, B, C)
- 52 assorted squares, each 3½" x 3½"

Light print (Fabric D)
- 12 squares, each 3½" x 3½"

Assorted Light, Medium, and Dark prints
- Cut each fat quarter into 2" x 22" strips*
- * You can cut strips as you need them when making the Fourpatch units if you wish.

Dark Floral Bouquet
- 4 lengthwise strips, each 6½" wide; you will trim later

Green print
- 7 strips, each 2½" wide, cut across the fabric width

Double Ninepatch Block Assembly

1. Sew 2" strips of light, medium, and dark prints into pairs. Press the seam toward the darker fabric in each unit. You will need at least 16 strip units that measure 20"-22" long. Crosscut into 2"-wide segments. You will need a total of 160 segments. Cut extra so you have some leeway for block layout.

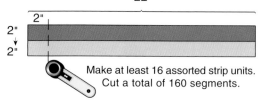

Make at least 16 assorted strip units.
Cut a total of 160 segments.

2. Sew segments together in pairs to make Fourpatch units. Make 80.

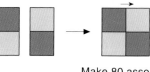

Make 80 assorted
Fourpatch units.

3. Arrange the Fourpatch units and 3½" squares to make a total of 16 scrappy blocks. Position Fourpatch units so they create a "chain" of color along one diagonal of each block as was done in the quilt shown—or make the blocks completely scrappy by random placement of the squares and Fourpatch units. Press all seams toward the large squares.

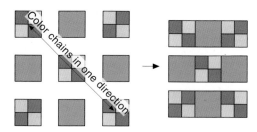

4. Sew the rows together to complete each block. Press seams in one direction.

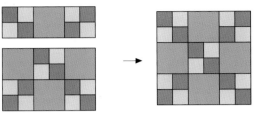

Scrappy Double Ninepatch
Make 16.

Quilt Top Assembly and Borders

1. Arrange the Double Ninepatch blocks with the setting squares and side setting triangles in diagonal rows. Sew together in rows and press all seams toward the setting squares and triangles. Add a small setting triangle to each corner. Press the seams toward the triangles.

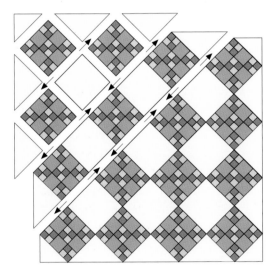

2. Measure the quilt top length through the center and add 18" (for mitered borders). Trim the 6½"-wide floral borders to this length.

3. Sew borders to quilt top following directions for mitered borders on pages 117 and 118. Press the seams toward the borders and miter the corners.

Finishing

1. Layer the quilt top, batting, and backing. Baste the layers together.

2. Mark and quilt as desired or follow the quilting suggestion below.

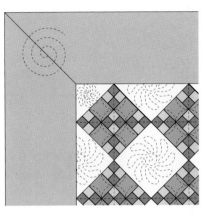

3. Trim the batting and backing even with the quilt top edges.

4. Sew the binding strips together to make one long piece. Bind the edges of the quilt.

5. Add a hanging sleeve if desired. Sign and date your finished quilt.

Home Decorating Hints

— Hang a photo of the quiltmaker in front of a quilt. This works well if you have old family photos or rescue anonymous relatives from antique shops. Many shops have old photos of interesting folks who need to be adopted.

— Hang an empty ornate picture frame or mirror over a quilt.

— For either of these, make sure the back is clean and smooth or glue felt over it.

— Hang with fine wire or clear fish line from ceiling or wall above quilt.

Garden Swirl

T'S FUN TO HAVE A TEA PARTY EVENT ONCE OR TWICE A YEAR WHEN quilters come together to share their work, brag about their children or grandchildren, tell stories, true or not, and eat lots of goodies. I found an article in *Home Arts Women's Weekly* from 1922 discussing tea parties, "Afternoon calling dresses are worn, heavy wraps are laid aside in a room for that purpose. The hats and gloves, however, are retained." 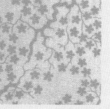 For our party everyone shows up with their hat firmly on their head and a yard of fabric, cut in any dimensions, wrapped prettily for the occasion. A number is drawn by each guest and determines the order in which the gifts are chosen. Each participant, in turn, may choose an unwrapped gift or one already opened by another. This gets a little dicey if a guest has become attached to her fabric, but the hat-and-gloves attire usually maintains decorum. At the last tea, I learned Betsy was getting a divorce and Bob was the best two hundred pounds she'd ever lost. Trish was sad about "Lottie's quilt story," so she told us that her research revealed that Lottie was not hurt badly when the horse fell on her, and Lottie's Pride went on to win the Kentucky Derby with Lottie astride—the first woman to win the Derby. Oh yes, Sue asked when the "reproducing fabric" was due at the store and Leah replied, "Nine months!"

Lovely fabrics in light, medium, and dark prints make this quilt sing.

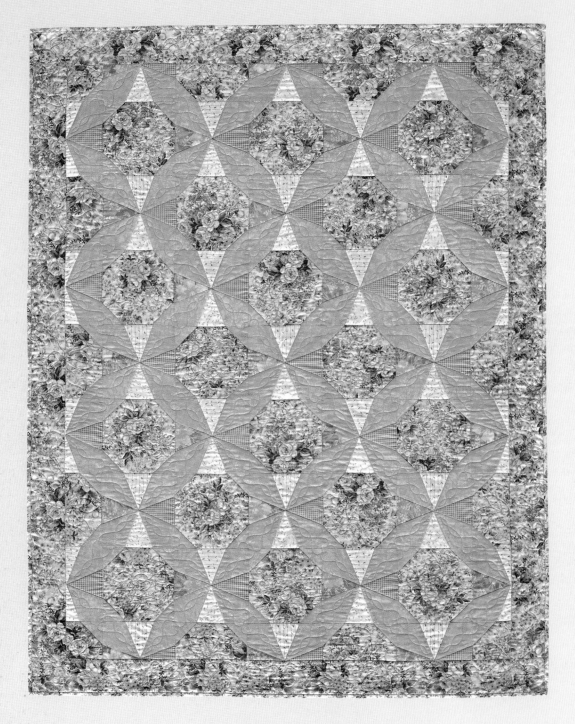

Garden Swirl

Soft color dances across this yummy quilt made with only two easy blocks—a template-free Floral Snowball and a template-cut Maltese Star block. Choose a tone-on-tone print for the Maltese Star corners that create the swirls around pretty bouquets of softly colored garden flowers.

DESIGNED BY: **Trish Carey**   QUILTED BY: **Sherry Rogers**
FINISHED SIZE: **50" x 67½"**   FINISHED BLOCK SIZE: **7½" x 7½"**

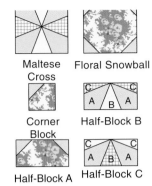

Maltese Cross Floral Snowball

Corner Block Half-Block B

Half-Block A Half-Block C

Directions for "Basic Quiltmaking Techniques" begin on page 114.

Cutting Instructions

Use Templates A, B, and C on page 57. Cut all strips across the fabric width from selvage to selvage, unless otherwise directed. Cut the floral borders first, then cut the remaining pieces from the remaining fabric.

Floral Bouquet
- 2 strips, each 4" x 53", and 2 strips each 4" x 72", cut lengthwise for the borders; you will trim to size later
- 18 squares, each 8" x 8", for Floral Snowball blocks
- 10 rectangles, each 4¼" x 8", for the half-blocks
- 4 squares, each 4¼" x 4¼", for the corner squares
- 2½"-wide strips (to total 7 yards) for binding

Pink tone-on-tone print
- 7 strips, each 2¾" wide; crosscut 96 squares, each 2¾" x 2¾"
- 96 Template A

Light coordinating prints
- 20 Template B from each print for a total of 40
- 8 Template C from each print for a total of 16

Dark coordinating prints
- 21 Template B from each print for a total of 42
- 6 Template C from each print for a total of 12

Snowball Block and Half-Block A Assembly

1. Draw a diagonal line on the wrong side of each 2¾" pink square.

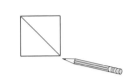

2. Place a pink square face down on the right side in each corner of each 8" floral bouquet square, making sure that the drawn lines are correctly positioned. Stitch on each drawn line. Trim each corner ¼" from the stitching and press seams toward the corners.

Floral Snowball
Make 18.

3. Repeat with the floral rectangles and the remaining pink squares, placing squares as shown.

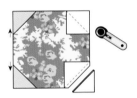

Half-Block A
Make 10.

4. Position a pink square on one corner of each of the four 4¼" floral squares. Stitch and trim as you did for the Floral Snowballs.

Corner Block
Make 4.

Maltese Cross Block Assembly

1. Sew each piece A to a piece B and press the seam allowances toward A.

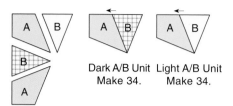

Dark A/B Unit
Make 34.

Light A/B Unit
Make 34.

2. Alternating light and dark triangles B as shown, sew the A/B units together in pairs to make a total of 34 A/B units. Press all seams toward A. Set remaining A/B units aside for the half-blocks.

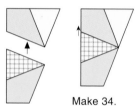

Make 34.

3. Make 17 blocks by sewing block halves together, matching the seams at the center of each block. Press seams in one direction.

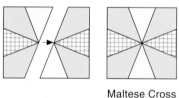

Maltese Cross
Make 17.

Half-Blocks B and C Assembly

1. Using the remaining pink pieces, make 6 light Unit A/B/A and 8 dark Unit A/B/A. Press seams toward A.

Light Unit A/B/A
Make 6.

Dark Unit A/B/A
Make 8.

2. Add 2 dark Piece C to each light A/B/A and 2 light Piece C to each dark A/B/A. Press seams toward Piece A.

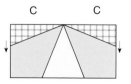 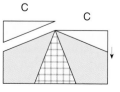

Half-Block B
Make 6.

Half-Block C
Make 8.

Quilt Top Assembly and Borders

1. Following the diagram, arrange the blocks, half-blocks and corner blocks in the number of required horizontal rows, taking care to place the dark triangles in the horizontal position across the rows. Sew the blocks together in rows and press the seams toward the Snowball blocks in each row.

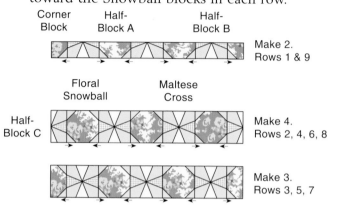

Corner
Block

Half-
Block A

Half-
Block B

Make 2.
Rows 1 & 9

Floral
Snowball

Maltese
Cross

Half-
Block C

Make 4.
Rows 2, 4, 6, 8

Make 3.
Rows 3, 5, 7

2. Referring to the quilt plan, arrange the rows in numerical order and sew together, matching seams carefully. Press seams in one direction.

3. Measure the quilt top length through the center and trim 2 floral bouquet border strips to this measurement. Sew to the long edges of the quilt top. Press the seams toward the border.

4. Measure the quilt top width through the center, including the border strips you just added, and cut border strips to this measurement. Sew to the top and bottom edges of the quilt top. Press the seams toward the borders.

Finishing

1. Layer the quilt top, batting, and backing. Baste the layers together.

2. Mark and quilt as desired or stitch in the ditch of the seams as shown, do free-form stitching in the Snowballs—loosely following the floral motifs—and quilt a small design in the pink areas. Quilt borders as desired.

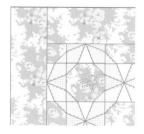

3. Trim the batting and backing even with the quilt top edges.
4. Sew the binding strips together to make one long piece. Bind the edges of the quilt.
5. Add a hanging sleeve if desired. Sign and date your finished quilt.

Home Decorating Hints

— Bring out all of your old china pieces. Nohing has to match.

— Hang a beautiful quilt behind your tea table.

— Use an inexpensive lace curtain for a tablecloth.

Garden Swirl Templates

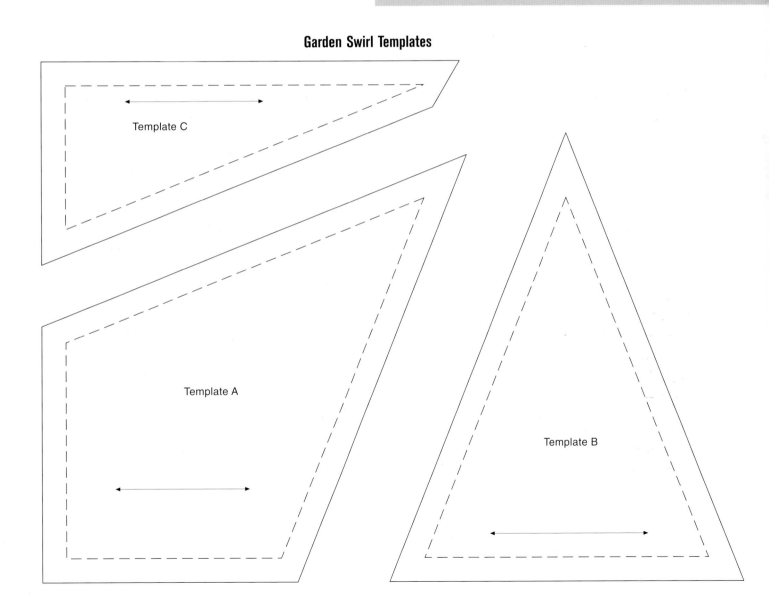

Template C

Template A

Template B

Hidden Meadows

*T*RISH CAREY MADE THIS QUILT USING MANY NINETEENTH CENTURY reproduction floral fabrics. It is wonderfully elegant so we wanted a unique piece of furniture to show it off. Price was a consideration so we decided on the popular "Shabby Chic" look. Dictionary definitions include: shabby (shăb-ē): worn-out; and chic (shēk): fashionable, smartly stylish. In my day, we pronounced it "chick" and nothing in one's house went shabby! I remember spending months removing coats of sticky paint from forlorn furniture to get the perfect finish I wanted. ✑ Now you can find a tragic little piece, take it home, brush it off and call it marvelous. Antique silver should not be polished; paint should not be stripped; beds can just be fluffed. As a "young Senior," it works for me! We scoured thrift shops, garage sales, consignment stores, and antique malls. When we saw the shoddy little French daybed in this photo, we let out a scream—in unison. It was tarnished, chipped, all the worse for wear—it was perfect!

Large floral prints combine with smaller scale patterns to blend together into a "dreamy" quilt.

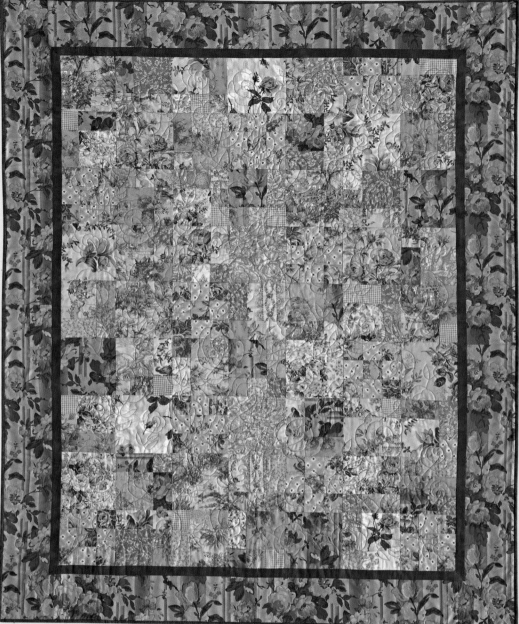

dden Meadows

dark floral & binding
-dark green print
light floral - yellow print
inner border - lime, aqua
& pink stripe
Outer border - large green
floral
Backing - large aqua
floral

re hidden throughout this mélange of floral blocks, some
g fabrics for this inviting meadow of flowers? Choose floral fat
er so that each block seems to "melt" into the next. Choose a
ller floral prints. Include a toile or two and small checks or
quilts made from this pattern could possibly look the same!

rish Carey   QUILTED BY: **Maradie Birmingham**

E: **55" x 67"**   FINISHED BLOCK SIZE: **6" x 6"**

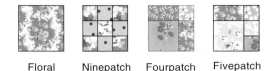

Floral Onepatch · Ninepatch · Fourpatch · Fivepatch

Directions for "Basic Quiltmaking Techniques" begin on page 114.

Cutting Instructions

Cut strips across the width of the fabric from selvage to selvage, unless otherwise directed.

Light floral
- for Ninepatches, 4 strips, each 2½" wide

Dark floral
- for Ninepatches, 5 strips, each 2½" wide

Large Floral Bouquet
- 4 strips, each 5¾" wide, cut the length of the fabric; cut some of the pieces for the One-, Four-, and Fivepatch blocks from the remaining fabric if desired, and include 1 or 2 of the Onepatch squares. *Note:* Two of the borders in the quilt on page 60 were cut crosswise to keep the stripe in the fabric consistent. Unless your fabric is 45" or wider, you must piece crosswise border strips to get the correct length.

Assorted Floral Bouquet prints
- 18 assorted squares, each 6½" x 6½", for Floral Onepatch blocks
- 35 assorted squares, each 4½" x 4½", for Four- and Fivepatch blocks
- 48 assorted rectangles, each 2½" x 4½", for Four- and Fivepatch blocks
- 79 squares, each 2½" x 2½"

Dark green
- 8 strips, each 1½" wide, for inner borders
- 7 strips, each 2½" wide, for binding

Ninepatch Block Assembly

1. Using the 2½"-wide strips of the light and dark florals, make 2 of Strip Unit A. Press the seams toward the dark floral strips. Crosscut a total of 20 segments, each 2½" wide.

2½"

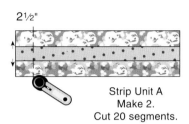

Strip Unit A
Make 2.
Cut 20 segments.

2. Using the remaining light and dark floral strips, make 1 Strip Unit B. Press the seams toward the dark floral strip.

2½"

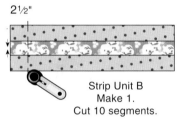

Strip Unit B
Make 1.
Cut 10 segments.

3. Arrange the segments from steps 1 and 2 to make 10 Ninepatch blocks. Sew the segments together for each block and press seams in one direction.

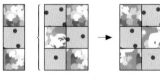

Ninepatch
Make 10.

Four- and Fivepatch Block Assembly

1. Make 22 three-patch units, using assorted 2½" floral squares. Press the seams in one direction.

Make 22.

Hidden Meadows

Fabric Requirements
44"-wide fabrics

- Assorted Floral Bouquet prints in colors of similar value for One-, Four-, and Fivepatch blocks: 12 or more fat quarters
- Dark floral for Ninepatch blocks - ½ yd.
- Light floral for Ninepatch blocks - ⅜ yd.
- Dark green solid or tone-on-tone print for inner border and binding - 1 yd.
- Large Floral Bouquet for outer border and blocks - 2½ yds.
- Backing - 3½ yds.
- Batting - 60" x 72" piece

2. Sew a 2½" x 4½" rectangle to each 4½" square. Press the seams toward the large square in each unit.

Make 35.

3. Sew a 2½" square to each of the remaining 2½" x 4½" rectangles.

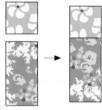

Make 13.

4. Make 22 Fivepatch blocks and press the seams in the direction of the small arrow.

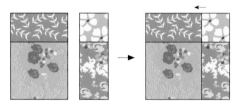

Fivepatch
Make 22.

5. Make 13 Fourpatch blocks and press the seams in the direction of the arrow.

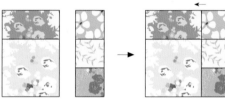

Fourpatch
Make 13.

Quilt Top Assembly

1. Following the quilt layout or positioning blocks as desired, arrange the Floral One-, Four-, Five- and Ninepatch blocks into 9 rows of 7 blocks each. Take care to position blocks so colors flow from one into the next. Turn blocks as necessary to create the desired effect. Sew the blocks together in rows and press the seams in opposite directions from row to row.

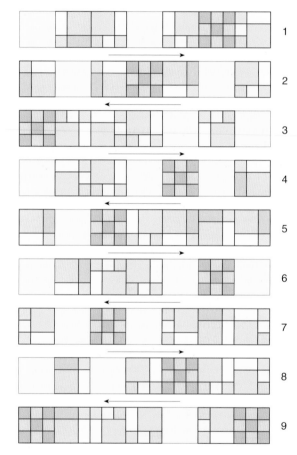

2. Sew the dark green border strips together end-to-end in pairs, using a diagonal seam. Press the seams open.

3. Sew a dark green border strip to one long edge of each of the four 5¾"-wide floral border strips. Press the seams toward the green border. Trim excess green border even with floral strip

4. Measure the quilt top length through the center and add 15½". Cut border strips to this measurement. Sew to the long edges of the quilt top as directed for borders with mitered corners on pages 117 and 118. Press the seams toward the green inner borders.

5. Measure the quilt top width through the center, including the border strips you just added, and cut border strips to this measurement plus 3". Sew to the top and bottom edges of the quilt top.

6. Miter the border corners and trim as needed, leaving a ¼"-wide seam allowance. Press open.

Finishing

1. Layer the quilt top, batting, and backing. Baste the layers together.

2. Mark and quilt as desired or quilt in an overall floral pattern similar to the one below. If border fabric has large floral motifs, quilt around individual flowers.

3. Trim the batting and backing even with the quilt top edges.

4. Sew the binding strips together to make one long piece. Bind the edges of the quilt.

5. Add a hanging sleeve if desired. Sign and date your finished quilt.

Home Decorating Hints

⌐ Odd little tables are inexpensive and are easy to find.

⌐ Stack small shabby footstools for side tables. Paint them or sand them for a shabby look.

⌐ For a little luxury, use lots of pillows in a variety of prints and shapes. You can sew scraps together to make pillow covers, and look for antique petit point or needlepoint pillows to add to the mix. Prize these little gems for the time and talent it took to make them.

Le Jardin

LARRY SHECKMAN IS A SALESMAN *PAR EXCELLENCE* AND SELLS our In The Beginning line of fabric to quilt shops in parts of the Eastern United States. He handles many lines of cloth from other companies and one of them consists of exclusive designer dress fabric. We always "ooh and aah" at the gorgeous silks, rayons, and linens he produces from his bags. At the last Market

he had a stunning Italian floral linen that I thought would look elegant in a wallhanging. No sooner had I mentioned the idea than his lovely wife Julie volunteered to create an original quilt for this book. ∞ Julie met Larry while she was managing a quilt shop in Florida several years ago. (Yes, romance is alive and well in the quilt business!) Since their marriage and her move to Philadelphia she has designed quilts for fabric companies as well as several major quilt publications. ∞ The piece Julie designed for us is beautiful and sophisticated. This quilt is about keeping an open mind when considering your fabric choices and accessories. If you want chintz, linen, flannel, or jacquard—use them. If you want buttons, beads, jewelry, or paint for accents—go for it! ∞ Quiltmaking is about your creativity and sense of uniqueness, not about following arbitrary conservative rules. Don't ever limit yourself.

A beautiful linen floral from Italy makes this quilt an elegant addition to your home.

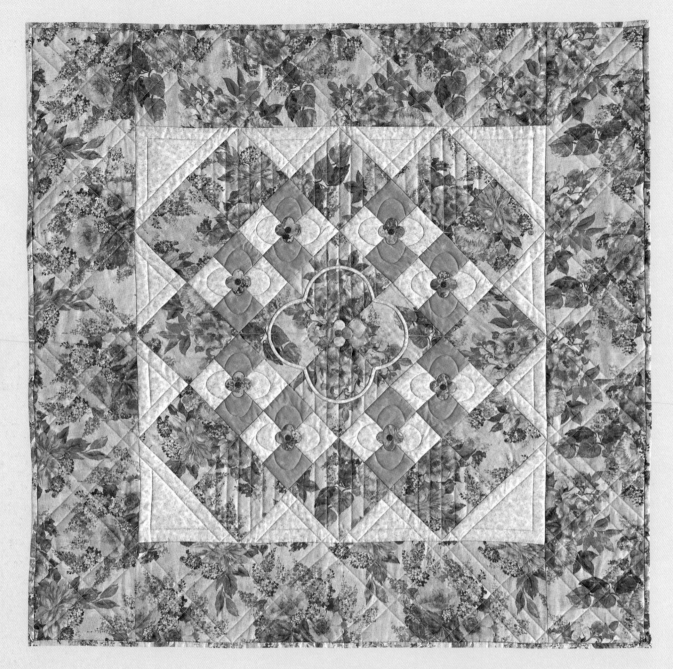

Le Jardin

Julie chose a large floral bouquet to create a lovely garden walk, embellished with appliquéd posies and a Celtic ring. The linen floral bouquet fabric forms a beautiful border to frame the on-point setting of simple Fourpatch and floral blocks. The resulting quilt is an inviting place to rest your eyes and delight in the glory of a simple but elegant garden.

DESIGNED AND QUILTED BY: **Julie Sheckman**

FINISHED SIZE: **51" x 51"**   FINISHED BLOCK SIZE: **6" x 6"**

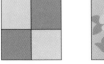

Fourpatch   Floral Onepatch

Directions for "Basic Quiltmaking Techniques" begin on page 114.

Cutting Instructions

Cut all strips across the width of the fabric from selvage to selvage, unless otherwise directed.

Floral Bouquet fabric
- 3 strips, 6½" wide; crosscut 16 squares, each 6½" x 6½"
- 2 strips, 9" x 36", for top and bottom borders*
- 2 strips, 9" x 54", for side borders*
- * Cut lengthwise extra long; you will trim later

Green tone-on-tone print
- 2 strips, each 3½" wide

Ecru tone-on-tone print
- 2 strips, each 3½" wide
- 2 squares, each 10" x 10"; cut twice diagonally for 8 side setting triangles*
- 2 squares, each 9¾"x 9¾"; cut once diagonally for 4 corner triangles*
- * These are oversize; you will trim later

Backing and binding
- 54" x 54" piece*
- 2⅜"-wide bias strips to make 5¾" yds.
- * You will need to piece the backing if you are using 44"-wide floral fabric.

Fourpatch Block Assembly

1. With right sides together, stitch each green tone-on-tone strip to an ecru tone-on-tone strip. Press the seams toward the green fabric in each strip-pieced unit. Cut a total of 16 segments, each 3½"-wide, from the strip units.

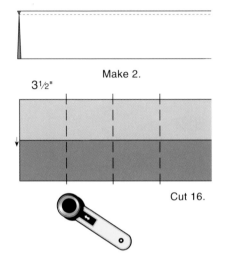

Make 2.

3½"

Cut 16.

2. Arrange the segments in pairs to create 8 Fourpatch blocks. Sew segments together for each block and press the seam in one direction.

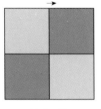

Make 8.

Le Jardin

Fabric Requirements
Floral Bouquet print

2⅜ yds. 54"-wide linen floral* OR 2¾ yds. 44"-wide cotton floral
* If you are using a linen floral, decide whether you want your finished quilt to be washable. If so, test wash a scrap of the linen for colorfastness and to make sure you like the resulting hand. It may be difficult to remove wrinkles in some linens as well. Since linen shrinks considerably in the wash, you will need additional yardage if you choose to pre-wash the linen. I suggest dry cleaning, the same as you would a fine linen garment.
- Green tone-on-tone print - ¼ yd.
- Ecru tone-on-tone print - ⅝ yd.
- Backing - 1¾ yds. 54"-wide linen floral OR 3¼ yds. 44"-wide fabric. You will need to piece the backing if using 44"-wide fabric.
- Batting - 54" x 54" piece
- Binding - ½ yd. for bias-cut binding
- Paper-backed fusible web - ¼ yd.
- Optional: Red, green, and ecru cordonnet thread for appliqués

Quilt Top Assembly

1. Following the quilt layout, arrange the Fourpatch blocks with the floral squares and setting triangles in diagonal rows.

2. Sew the blocks and side setting triangles together in rows. You will add corner triangles later. Press the seam allowances in opposite directions from row to row.

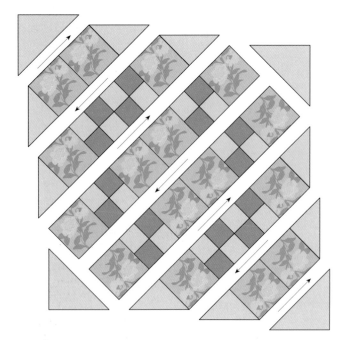

Tip: *If your linen fabric tends to ravel a lot, treat the edge with a thin line of seam sealant such as Fray Check™.*

3. Sew the rows together and press seam allowances in one direction. Sew a corner triangle to each corner of the quilt top. Trim side and corner triangles as necessary. Press seams toward the corner triangles.

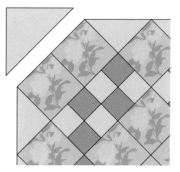

Add corner triangles last.

4. Measure the length of the quilt top through the center and trim two 9"-wide borders to match this measurement. Sew borders to opposite edges of the quilt top and press the seams toward the borders.

5. Measure the width of the quilt top through the center, including the borders you just added, and trim the remaining 9"-wide border strips to this measurement. Sew to the top and bottom edges of the quilt top. Press the seams toward the borders.

6. Press the completed quilt top and machine baste around the outer edge to stabilize the top while you add the appliqués.

Appliqués

Use Templates A, B, and C on page 71.

1. Apply fusible web to the wrong side of enough floral fabric scraps for 8 flowers, and to a small scrap large enough for 1 flower of each of the two tone-on-tone prints.

2. Using Template A, trace 8 flowers onto the fusible-web transfer paper on the floral fabric. Trace 1 flower each onto the green and ecru prints. Cut out each appliqué. Cut the green and ecru flowers into four petals each.

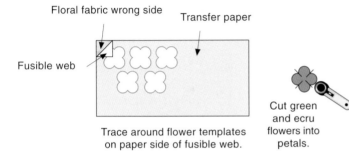

Floral fabric wrong side Transfer paper

Fusible web

Trace around flower templates on paper side of fusible web.

Cut green and ecru flowers into petals.

3. Position a floral appliqué at the center of each Fourpatch block. Fuse in place.

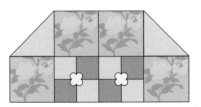

Fuse flowers in place at Fourpatch centers.

4. Arrange 2 green and 2 ecru petals in alternating fashion to create a flower at the center of the quilt top. Fuse in place.

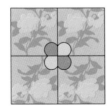

Quilt center

5. From floral fabric leftovers, cut 9 red flower centers, using Template B. Fuse one in place at the center of each appliquéd flower.

Cut and fuse a center to each flower.

6. Optional: Machine straight stitch around the outer edge of each flower and flower center with red, green, or ecru cordonnet thread. You can do this later, when you do the quilting, if you prefer.

Paper-Patch Appliqué

Make a paper template of each appliqué shape without seam allowance. Inexpensive materials for this include old Christmas or greeting cards or those irritating advertising pullouts in magazines.

1. Pin the paper patches to the wrong side of the appliqué fabric. Pin from the right side of the fabric to prevent the thread from catching as you baste from the wrong side. Cut out the appliqué shapes, adding a ¼"-wide seam allowance all around.

2. Turn the seam allowance over onto the paper and baste.

Note: Clip the seam allowance on curves and sharp dips. For circles, baste around the outer edge of the circle fabric. Pull the thread to gather the fabric tightly around the paper template. Appliqué the circle to the background fabric, three-quarters of the way around. Remove the basting stitches and paper template (use tweezers if necessary); fold under the circle's remaining seam allowance and finish appliquéing the circle.

7. To mark the position for the appliquéd Celtic motif at the center of the quilt, trace Template C, cut out and position on one floral block at the center of the quilt. Lightly trace around the outer edge. Repeat on the remaining blocks.

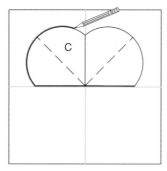

Trace around Template C
to mark bias placement.

8. Cut ¾"-wide bias strips from the ecru tone-on-tone fabric scraps. Join strips as needed to make a piece 36" long.

Home Decorating Hints

— Make several large pillows with the linen print to throw on a sofa or chair, or find a coordinating decorator print that accentuates a color in the wallhanging. *Très chic!*

— Notice the use of small lemons and limes in the hurricane candleholders. Use fruits along with floral arrangements when entertaining.

9. Fold strip in half lengthwise, with wrong sides together; stitch ¼" from the raw edges. Trim seam to ⅛". Center the stitching on the back side of the fabric tube and press lightly.

Center seamline
on back side of
bias fabric tube.

10. Center the bias strip over the positioning line on the quilt top and pin in place, mitering the corners as needed. Steam press lightly to help shape the bias to the curve. Hand or machine stitch in place.

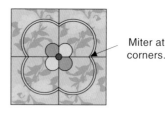

Miter at corners.

11. Optional: Machine straight stitch around the inner and outer edges of the bias strip using ecru or green cordonnet for emphasis—or wait to do this when you do the quilting.

Finishing

1. Layer the quilt with batting and backing.
2. Baste the quilt layers together. Mark and quilt as desired. Julie quilted around each appliqué flower in the Fourpatch blocks, and stitched parallel lines spaced 1" apart on the diagonal of each floral block.

Floral Onepatch   Fourpatch   Setting triangle

3. Trim the excess batting and backing even with the quilt top edges.
4. Sew the bias strips for the binding together to create one long strip. Bind the quilt edges.
5. Add a hanging sleeve if desired. Sign and date your finished quilt.

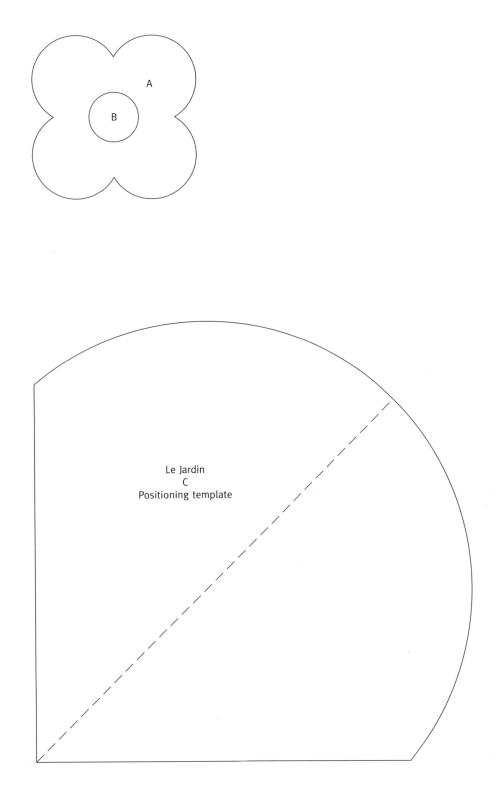

A

B

Le Jardin
C
Positioning template

A Walk in the Garden

I N THE SPRING OF 2000, VICKI HURST, OUR WHOLESALE MANAGER, and I went to International Quilt Market in Strasbourg, France. After the show was finished, we joined a group of twenty quilters on a barge trip through some of the French canals. We visited textile exhibits, quilt shows, and the largest textile museum in the world at Mulhouse, France. ✺ 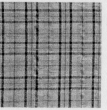 When we first boarded our floating hotel, the crew inquired if we would want wine with our meals, as they were not familiar with the "Quaker life." As we tried to explain that we were quilters not Quakers the word "quackers" somehow came up. We said no, that's the sound ducks make and the crew was even more puzzled. After lots of laughter and confusion, someone said "patch-workers" and they understood. We also explained that many American "patchworkers" like a little wine now and then and the problem was solved. ✺ Each morning our guide, Marciel, would arrive in a bus to take us on a tour before lunch. One day we explored a large cave and studied some fossils. Marciel commented that he had collected fossils as a child. "And now you just drive them around," interjected one of our group. ✺ Everyone we met was so patient and friendly, including the French patchworkers, who were so stylish with their lovely silk scarves tied around their necks. I've tried—but I look like an old Camp Fire girl. Guess it must be a "French thing!"

The addition of a plaid fabric scattered throughout cuts the sweetness of this quilt.

A Walk in the Garden

In this colorful variation on the traditional Jacob's Ladder pattern, scrappy Fourpatch
stepping stones create the pathways through and around the flower patches. This quilt
is constructed in diagonal rows of pieced units alternating with floral squares—rather
than with blocks. The overall pattern emerges only after the top is completed.

DESIGNED BY: SHARON YENTER

QUILTED BY: LAURIE SHIFRIN   FINISHED SIZE: 51⅜" x 51⅜"

Directions for "Basic Quiltmaking Techniques" begin on page 114.

Cutting Instructions

Floral Bouquet fabric on blue background
- 3 strips, each 7⅝" wide; crosscut 13 squares, each 7⅝" x 7⅝", for the Floral Squares

Assorted light, medium, and dark prints
- 1¾"-wide strips, cut parallel to the longest dimension of each fat quarter, for the Fourpatch Units. Cut at least 30 strips; cut more if needed

Assorted light prints
- 54 assorted 2⅝" squares; cut each once diagonally for a total of 108 small triangles for Fourpatch Units
- 21 assorted 4⅞" squares; cut each twice diagonally for a total of 84 large triangles for Fourpatch Units

Medium print (tan)
- 3 strips, each 4" wide, cut parallel to the longest dimension of the fat quarter; crosscut 12 squares, each 4" x 4"; cut a fourth strip if necessary

Red print
- 4 squares, each 5" x 5", for border corners

Gold plaid
- 5 strips, each 1½" wide, cut across the fabric width for inner borders

Blue tone-on-tone print
- 4 lengthwise strips, each 4" x 46", for outer border (cut extra long; you will trim later)
- 6 lengthwise strips, each 2½" x 46", for binding
- 2 squares, each 9½" x 9½"; cut twice diagonally for 8 side setting triangles (cut oversize; you will trim later)
- 2 squares, each 3⅜" x 3⅜"; cut once diagonally for 4 corner units

Fourpatch Unit Assembly

1. Sew light, medium, and dark 1¾" strips together in pairs in assorted combinations to make a minimum of 15 strip sets. Press the seam toward the darkest fabric in each strip unit. Crosscut a total of 144 segments.

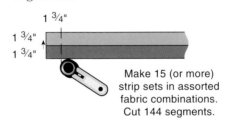

Make 15 (or more) strip sets in assorted fabric combinations. Cut 144 segments.

2. Arrange the segments to make 72 scrappy Fourpatch Units. Sew the segments together for each unit and press the seams in one direction.

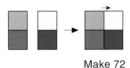

Make 72 Fourpatch Units in assorted fabric combinations.

3. Sew a large light triangle to one edge of each Fourpatch, positioning triangles as shown. Press the seams toward the triangles.

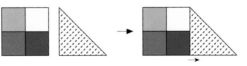

Make 72.

4. Arrange Fourpatch/triangle strips in pairs and sew together.

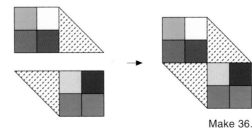

Make 36.

A Walk in the Garden

Fabric Requirements
44"-wide fabrics

Note: Fat quarters measure 18" x 20"-22" before preshrinking.
- Floral Bouquet fabric on blue background for Floral setting squares - ⅞ yd.
- Assorted light, medium, and dark prints for Fourpatch Units (blues, golds, reds) - 12 or more fat quarters or scraps totaling 2 yds.
- Assorted light prints for triangles in Fourpatch Units - 6 or more fat quarters or scraps totaling ⅞ yd.
- Medium print (tan) for corner squares - 1 fat quarter
- Red print for border corners - 1 fat quarter
- Blue tone-on-tone print for borders, setting triangles and binding - 1½ yds.*
* If fabric measures less than 41" wide after preshrinking and removing selvages, you will need an additional ⅜ yard of fabric.
- Gold plaid for inner border - ⅜ yd.
- Backing - 3⅜ yd.
- Batting - 56" x 56" piece

5. Make the required number of each Fourpatch Unit, adding small light corner triangles and large light triangles as required for each one.

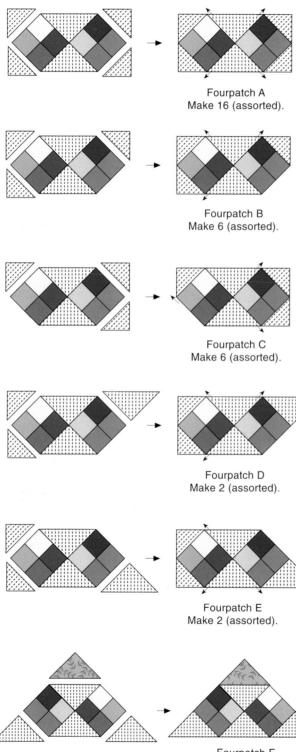

Fourpatch A
Make 16 (assorted).

Fourpatch B
Make 6 (assorted).

Fourpatch C
Make 6 (assorted).

Fourpatch D
Make 2 (assorted).

Fourpatch E
Make 2 (assorted).

Fourpatch F
Corner Units
Make 4.

Quilt Top Assembly

1. Arrange Fourpatch A, B, C Units, large floral squares, 4" squares, and side setting triangles in the 9 rows shown. Sew the pieces together in each row and press seams toward the floral squares, setting triangles, and small squares.

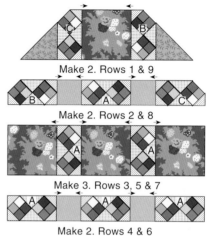

Make 2. Rows 1 & 9

Make 2. Rows 2 & 8

Make 3. Rows 3, 5 & 7

Make 2. Rows 4 & 6

2. Sew the rows together in numerical order and add a corner unit to each short end. Press seams in one direction.

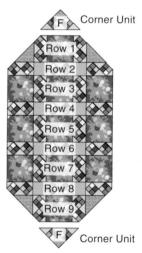

F Corner Unit
Row 1
Row 2
Row 3
Row 4
Row 5
Row 6
Row 7
Row 8
Row 9
F Corner Unit

3. Arrange and assemble the remaining rows as shown. Press seams toward the floral squares, setting triangles, and 4" squares.

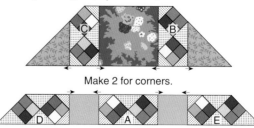

Make 2 for corners.

Make 2 for corners.

4. Make two corner units with the remaining Fourpatch F Units and the rows from step 3. Press seams in one direction. Sew one to each remaining corner of the quilt top.

Borders

1. Using diagonal seams, sew the 1½" plaid inner border strips together to make one long piece. Cut into 4 pieces the same length as the blue outer border strips.

2. Sew each plaid inner border strip to a blue outer border strip. Press the seam toward the plaid strip in each unit.

3. Measure the quilt top length through the center and trim all 4 inner/outer border strips to this measurement. Sew a border to 2 opposite edges of the quilt top. Press the seams toward the plaid borders.

4. Sew a 5" red corner square to each short end of the remaining border strips. Press the seams toward the squares. Sew a border to the top and bottom edges of the quilt top. Press the seams toward the plaid borders.

Make 2.

Finishing

1. Layer the quilt top, batting, and backing. Baste the layers together.

2. Mark and quilt as desired or follow the quilting suggestion below.

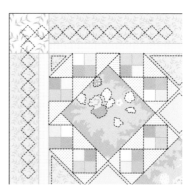

3. Trim the batting and backing even with the quilt top edges.

4. Sew the binding strips together to make one long piece. Bind the edges of the quilt.

5. Add a hanging sleeve if desired. Sign and date your finished quilt.

Home Decorating Hints

Use antique sewing cabinets for end tables or occasional tables. They are wonderful accents in a small room and are great collector's items.

Unique items add personality to a room. The Godey fashion print in this photo was just $12 in a consignment store.

Log Cabin Garden

WHEN I OPENED IN THE BEGINNING FABRICS IN 1977, THE LOG Cabin quilt was our most popular pattern. Every day we would help plan several of them for pleased customers. ✿ The Log Cabin pattern is probably the oldest patchwork in existence. In the 1930s, several remnants of the tattered design were found in an ancient Egyptian tomb. It is supposed that garments constructed from this type of configuration were worn by royalty around 3000 B.C. Isn't the continuity exciting? ✿ It's such fun watching new quilters discover this pattern. Everything old is new again!

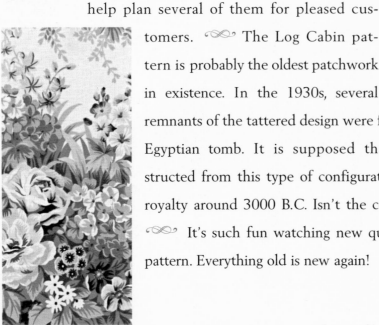

A traditional favorite,

blue and white,

combine for a novel

lattice idea.

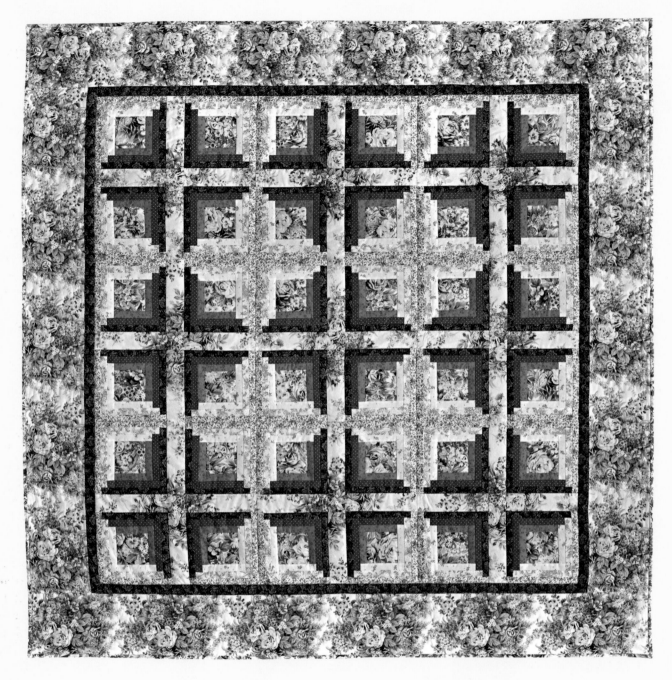

Log Cabin Garden

Lattice strips at the crossroads, carefully cut to showcase the floral bouquet,
surround traditional Log Cabin blocks in this interesting variation.
Choose three dark prints that graduate in color depth and three light prints
that graduate in print density to duplicate the colorwashed effect in each block.

DESIGNED BY: **Sharon Yenter**   QUILTED BY: **Maradie Birmingham**
FINISHED SIZE: **71½" x 71½"**   FINISHED BLOCK SIZE: **8" x 8"**
FINISHED BLOCK SET WITH SASHING: **18" x 18"**

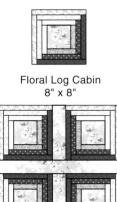

Floral Log Cabin
8" x 8"

18" x 18"

Directions for "Basic Quiltmaking Techniques" begin on page 114.

Cutting Instructions

Cut all strips across the width of the fabric from selvage to selvage.

Dark #1
- 9 strips, each 1¼" wide

Dark #2
- 11 strips, each 1¼" wide

Dark #3
- 14 strips, each 1¼" wide
- 8 strips, each 1¾"; set aside for the inner borders

Light #1
- 10 strips, each 1¼" wide

Light #2
- 13 strips, each 1¼" wide

Light #3
- 16 strips, each 1¼" wide

Cutting the Floral Bouquet Pieces

Cut pieces in the order given.

1. From the floral bouquet, cut a 76" long piece and set aside for the outer borders.
2. For the lattice, cut 9 strips, each 2½" wide, cutting across the remaining fabric width. From each of these strips, cut 2 strips, each 2½" x 8½", planning the cut so one end of each strip is in the densest portion of a bouquet.

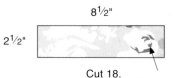

8½"

2½"

Cut 18.

Dense floral
at one end

3. From remaining long strips cut in step 2, cut 9 more lattice strips, each 2½" x 18½", planning the cuts so that the bouquet is centered in each strip.

Dense floral centered.

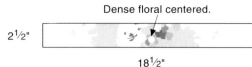

2½"

18½"

Cut 9.

4. Cut 36 squares, each 4" x 4". Cut each square so that it is densely filled with flowers.

4"

4"

Cut 36.

Log Cabin Garden

Fabric Requirements
44"-wide fabrics

- Large-scale Floral Bouquet for block centers, sashing, borders, and binding - 4¼ yds.*
- Dark print #1 for blocks - ½ yd.
- Dark print #2 for blocks - ½ yd.
- Dark print #3 for blocks and inner border - 1⅛ yds.
- Light print #1 - ½ yd.
- Light print #2 - ⅝ yd.
- Light print #3 - ¾ yd.
- Backing - 4½ yds.
- Batting - 76" x 76" piece

* Floral Bouquet fabric yardage is generous to allow for selective cutting. You may have excess fabric left over to add to your stash.

Log Cabin Block Assembly

All seam allowances are ¼" wide.

1. With raw edges even and right sides together, position a 4" floral bouquet square at one end of a strip of Dark #1. Stitch. Without breaking the stitching, leave a bit of space and add the next floral square to the strip; stitch. Continue adding and stitching squares in this manner, using additional Dark #1 strips as needed.

2. Trim the strips even with the edges of the squares. Press the seams toward the dark strips. Press all seams in this direction after each strip is added in the following steps.

3. Sew the resulting pieces to strips of Dark #1 in the same manner, making sure that all pieces are correctly positioned as shown in the diagram. Trim and press the seams toward the strips.

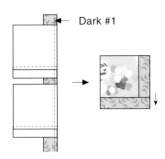

Dark #1

Note: *In this step and all that follow, the strip most recently added to the growing block should be at the bottom when you position it on the next strip. Press all strips away from the center square in each block.*

4. Rotate each piece and sew to strips of Light #1. Trim and press. Add a second strip of Light #1.

5. Add two strips of Dark #2, followed by two strips of Light #2.

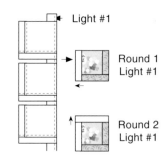

Round 1
Light #1

Round 2
Light #1

Round 4
Light #2

Round 3
Dark #2

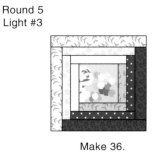

6. Complete each block with two strips of Dark #3, followed by two strips of Light #3.

Round 5
Light #3

Make 36.   Round 5
Dark #3

7. Arrange Log Cabins in groups of 4 with sashing strips as shown. Sew the blocks and short sashing together in rows and press the seams toward the sashing. Join the two rows of blocks to opposite edges of the long sashing. Press.

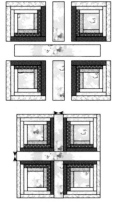

Make 9.

Quilt Top Assembly and Borders

1. Following the quilt plan, arrange the blocks in three rows of three blocks each. Sew the blocks together in rows and press the seams in one direction.

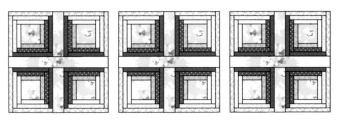

Make 3 rows.

2. Sew the rows together, matching seams carefully. Press seams in one direction.
3. Using a diagonal seam, sew the inner border strips together in pairs to make 4 long strips. Press seams open.
4. Measure the quilt top length through the center and trim 2 inner border strips to this measurement. Sew to the quilt top side edges. Press the seams toward the border.
5. Measure the quilt top width through the center, including the border strips you just added, and cut 2 inner border strips to this measurement. Sew to the top and bottom edges of the quilt top. Press the seams toward the borders.
6. Using the same method, measure the quilt for lengthwise borders and cut two lengthwise strips, each 7¾" wide, from the remaining floral bouquet fabric. Sew to the long edges of the quilt top.
7. Cut two floral borders for the top and bottom edges and sew to the quilt top.
8. From length of the fabric remaining from steps 6 and 7, cut 2½"-wide binding strips. If necessary, cut additional binding strips from the width of remaining floral bouquet fabric to get the length of binding you need.

Finishing

1. Layer the quilt top, batting, and backing. Baste the layers together.
2. Mark and quilt as desired.
3. Trim the batting and backing even with the quilt top edges.
4. Sew the binding strips together to make one long piece. Bind the edges of the quilt.
5. Add a hanging sleeve if desired. Sign and date your finished quilt.

Home Decorating Hints

— Use artificial ivy wound around the top of a four-poster bed, dresser, or chair to add freshness to a bedroom.

— Display a mirror, small collection, or picture inside an old window frame.

Chintz Squared

I REMEMBER SUMMER EVENINGS IN MY CHILDHOOD WHEN THE neighbor kids, my cousins, and I would roll down the slight embankment of cool green grass in my grandparents' front yard. We'd wait impatiently for the first star of the evening to appear in the dusky sky as we talked excitedly about the stars falling, Mount Rainier erupting, or how old we'd be in the year 2000. We'd giggle in disbelief at 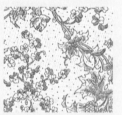 our old ages and wonder if we'd still be around. I figured I'd be sixty, tottering around and saying daffy things like the old woman in the purple house down our street. Imagine my surprise when the Millennium arrived and I was only fifty! ∽ Doesn't the song say, "There's no business like *Sew Business?*" One's birthdate can magically change in the same manner as a movie star…! Being happy with yourself and expressing your joy and talent in your quiltmaking can make you young at heart forever. This pattern is one of my favorites. I have been designing variations of it for years, but I never tire of its possibilities. Perhaps it will still be around in the twenty-second century!

Large bouquets and scattered flowers from the same fabric combine gracefully.

Chintz Squared

*Fabric and color placement create shadowplay in this easy but elegant
quilt. Notice how the darker triangles cast shadows across the dense
floral blocks, while the lighter triangles illuminate the remaining floral
blocks. Broderie perse bouquets fill the corners of this pretty garden setting.*

DESIGNED BY: **Sharon Yenter**   QUILTED BY: **Laurie Shifrin**

FINISHED SIZE: **52½" x 52½"**   FINISHED BLOCK SIZE: **7½" x 7½"**

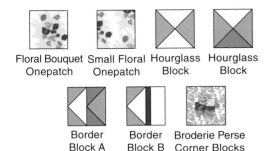

Floral Bouquet Onepatch   Small Floral Onepatch   Hourglass Block   Hourglass Block

Border Block A   Border Block B   Broderie Perse Corner Blocks

Directions for "Basic Quiltmaking Techniques" begin on page 114.

Cutting Instructions

Cut strips across the width of the fabric from selvage to selvage, unless otherwise directed.

Floral Bouquet

- 13 squares, each 8" x 8", with a bouquet centered in each square for blocks and broderie perse border corners
- 4 squares, each 8" x 8", with smaller-scale, more widely spaced flowers

Blue Accent

- 3 strips, each 8¾" wide; crosscut 9 squares, each 8¾" x 8¾"; cut each one twice diagonally for a total of 36 large triangles for the blocks and borders
- 3 strips, each 4⅝" wide; crosscut 20 squares, each 4⅝" x 4⅝"; cut each one once diagonally for a total of 40 small triangles for the border blocks

Fuchsia Accent

- 1 strip, 8¾" wide; crosscut 2 squares, each 8¾" x 8¾"; cut each one twice diagonally for a total of 8 triangles
- 2 strips, 4⅝" wide; crosscut 12 squares, each 4⅝" x 4⅝"; cut each one once diagonally for a total of 24 triangles

Light Accent

- 1 strip, 8" wide; crosscut 4 squares, each 8" x 8", for the broderie perse corner blocks
- 3 strips, each 8¾" wide; crosscut 9 squares, each 8¾" x 8¾"; cut each one twice diagonally for a total of 36 triangles for the blocks and border blocks
- 2 strips, each 3¼" wide, for the border blocks

Green Accent

- 2 strips, each 1½" wide, for the border blocks

Block and Border Construction

All seams are ¼" wide.

1. With right sides together, sew each of 16 light accent triangles to a large blue accent triangle. Press the seams toward the blue triangles.

Make 16.

2. Sew each of 8 blue accent triangles to a large fuchsia accent triangle. Press the seams toward the blue triangles.

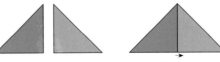

Make 8.

3. Arrange the triangle units in pairs to make 4 blue/white Hourglass blocks and 8 blue/light/fuchsia Hourglass blocks.

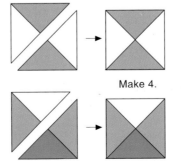

Make 4.

Make 8.

Chintz Squared

Fabric Requirements
44"-wide fabric

- Floral Bouquet* on blue ground - 1¼ yds.
- Blue Accent (tone-on-tone print) - 1⅜ yds.
- Light Accent (blue on white ground) - 1⅜ yds.
- Fuchsia Accent (tone-on-tone print) - ⅝ yd.
- Green Accent (solid or tone-on-tone) - ⅛ yd.
- Backing and Binding - 3½ yds.**
- Batting - 57" x 57" piece

* Floral Bouquets should measure approximately 7" across so they will be easy to center inside the 7½" perimeter of the 9 floral squares.

** If you prefer to use two different fabrics for binding and backing, you will need 3⅜ yds. for the backing and ½ yd. for straight-cut binding strips.

4. Sew a small blue accent triangle to each short side of each of the 20 remaining light accent triangles. Press the seams toward the blue triangles.

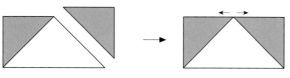

Make 20.

5. Sew a small fuchsia accent triangle to each short side of the 12 remaining large blue accent triangles. Press the seams toward the fuchsia triangles.

Make 12.

6. With right sides together, stitch each green strip to a light accent strip. Press the seam toward the green strip. Crosscut a total of 8 rectangles, each 8" long, for the border units.

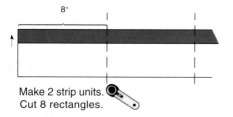

Make 2 strip units.
Cut 8 rectangles.

7. Sew each fuchsia/blue border unit to a light/blue border unit for a total of 12 Border Block A.

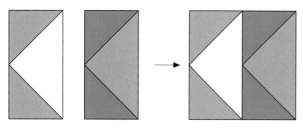

Border Block A
Make 12.

8. Sew each remaining light/blue border unit unit to a green/light rectangle for a total of 8 Border Block B.

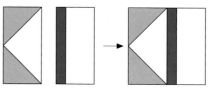

Border Block B
Make 8.

9. Following directions for broderie perse below, cut out a floral bouquet from each of the remaining 4 floral bouquet blocks, and appliqué to each of the 8" light accent squares.

Broderie Perse
Corner Blocks
Make 4.

Broderie Perse Appliqué

1. Select a motif from the printed fabric that will fit onto the area to be appliquéd.
2. Cut out the motif, adding a ¼"-wide seam allowance all around. If your motif has complicated edges, try to simplify the design for easier appliqué. If the background of your motif matches the background of the area to be appliquéd, allow a little of the appliqué background to show so you won't cut off the motif edges.
3. Pin or baste the motif onto the background. Turning under the ¼" seam allowance just before you take each stitch, appliqué the motif in place.

Note: If the motif you desire is too large to fit in the space, try to find a break in the pattern where you can cut it down to fit. (Sometimes, even if it overlaps the edges a bit in places, it will look all right.) If the motif is too small, try combining several small motifs to make a larger one. These could be several different designs or the same one repeated several times.

Quilt Top Assembly and Finishing

1. Arrange the floral bouquet squares, floral squares, hourglass blocks, and border blocks in the rows shown below. Sew the blocks together in each row and press all seams away from the floral bouquet and floral squares in each row.

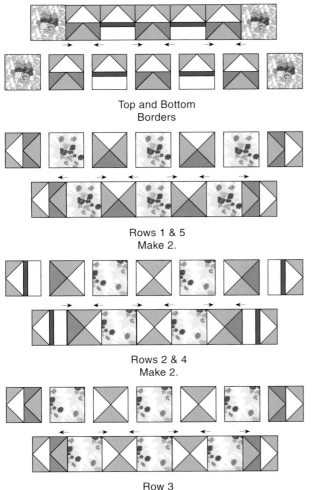

Top and Bottom Borders

Rows 1 & 5
Make 2.

Rows 2 & 4
Make 2.

Row 3
Make 1.

2. From the backing fabric, cut 2 lengths, each 57" long. Sew together, press the seam open, and trim the piece to 57" x 57". Set the remainder aside for the binding, if desired.
3. Layer the quilt with batting and backing.
4. Baste the quilt layers together. Mark and quilt as desired.

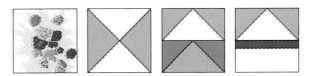

Quilt around floral motifs.　　Quilt pieced blocks in the ditch.

5. Trim the excess batting and backing even with the quilt top edges.
6. Sew the bias strips for the binding together to create one long strip. Bind the quilt edges.
7. Add a hanging sleeve if desired. Sign and date your quilt.

Home Decorating Hints

Create a vignette with a quilted wallhanging as a backdrop for flowers interspersed with votive candles. Match colors to your buffet or dining table. You could make room for coffee and dessert in an area like this. Notice the small stool used for height, hidden in the bouquets, colorful tins, and buckets containing flowers.

Oceans of Flowers

*I*N THE EARLY '90S, I WAS LOOKING AT SOME NICE BUT UNINTERESTING fabric and doing the "shop owner whine." "I don't like this color, don't like the styling…size…assortment…yadda yadda yadda." The Northcott salesman was losing patience with my negative comments and said sarcastically, "Yeah—if you're so smart why don't you design a line for us?" ∽∾ I looked at him unbelievingly and agreed to think about it. I spent the next two weeks preparing a portfolio and met with the principals of Northcott, Inc., a large Canadian fabric company based in Toronto. They liked my ideas and I signed a contract to design for them. ∽∾ I am forever grateful to them for the opportunity. It was a wonderful experience for me. I started with large decorator-type florals with coordinating fabrics and now continue to design these types of fabric for our own company, In The Beginning Fabrics. (Happily, Northcott remains our distributor in Canada.) ∽∾ This pattern showcases my large floral in the quilt borders. It's an Ocean Waves variation, but much easier than the original.

Small multi-colored tone-on-tone prints mix with large floral bouquets to create an intriguing wall quilt.

Oceans of Flowers

Flowers awash on the sea —what an enchanting image. The setting for the Floral Bouquet blocks creates an Ocean Waves variation design. It looks more complex than it is and is really easy to cut and piece. The placement of light and dark triangles in the alternating pinwheel blocks and the pieced side setting triangles make this quilt sparkle —the way sunlight dances on the water.

DESIGNED BY: **Sharon Yenter**   QUILTED BY: **Sherry Rogers and Margy Duncan**
FINISHED SIZE: **57¾" x 57¾"**   FINISHED BLOCK SIZE: **8" x 8"**

Pinwheel
Block A

Pinwheel
Block B

Square-in-a-square
Block C

Directions for "Basic Quiltmaking Techniques" begin on page 114.

Cutting Instructions

Floral Bouquet

- Selectively cut 4 border strips, each 7" x 60"

From the remaining fabric, cut

- 3 squares, each 12⅝" x 12⅝"; cut each twice diagonally to yield 12 side setting triangles
- 9 squares, each 6⅛" x 6⅛", for the centers of the Floral Square-in-a-Square blocks
- 2 squares, each 6⅜" x 6⅜"; cut each once diagonally for a total of 4 corner setting triangles

Assorted light fat quarters or scraps

- 38 squares, each 4⅞" x 4⅞", for the Pinwheel blocks; a few of these may be cut from the floral fabric scraps if desired
- 9 squares, each 4⅞" x 4⅞"; cut each once diagonally for a total of 18 half-square triangles for the Floral Square-in-a-Square blocks

Assorted dark fat quarters or scraps

- 38 squares, each 4⅞" x 4⅞", for the Pinwheel blocks and pieced side-setting triangles; a few of these may be cut from the floral fabric scraps if desired
- 9 squares, each 4⅞" x 4⅞"; cut each once diagonally for a total of 18 half-square triangles for the Floral Square-in-a-Square blocks

Tone-on-tone blue print

- 8 strips, each 1¼" wide, across the fabric width for the inner border

Binding fabric

- 6 strips, each 2½" wide, across the fabric width

Block and Setting Triangle Assembly

1. Place a light 4⅞" square right sides together with a dark 4⅞" square. On the wrong side of the light square, draw a line from corner to corner.

2. Stitch ¼" from the line on each side. Cut along the pencil line to make 2 half-square triangle units. Press the seam allowances toward the dark triangle in each unit. Repeat with 31 light and 31 dark squares to make a total of 64 half-square triangle units.

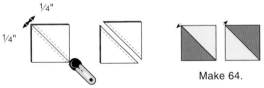

Make 64.

3. Arrange the half-square triangle units into 8 Pinwheel A and 8 Pinwheel B blocks, taking care to alternate and position the light and dark triangles as shown in the diagrams below.

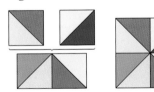

Pinwheel
Block A
Make 8.

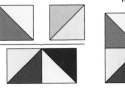

Pinwheel
Block B
Make 8.

4. Sew a light triangle to opposite sides of each 6⅛" square. Press the seams toward the triangles. Sew a dark triangle to each remaining side. Press toward the triangles.

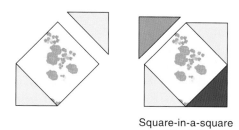

Square-in-a-square
Block C
Make 9.

5. Draw a diagonal line from corner to corner on each of the remaining 6 light and 6 dark 4⅞" squares. Place each square, right sides together, on a large floral side setting triangle and stitch on the drawn line. Trim, leaving a ¼"-wide seam allowance.

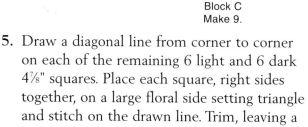

6. Press the seams toward the triangles.

 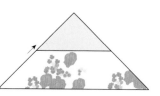

Dark side setting triangles
Make 6.

Light side setting triangles
Make 6.

Quilt Top Assembly

1. Arrange blocks and pieced side setting triangles in diagonal rows, taking care to position each block so that light and dark triangles alternate from block to block to create a sparkling effect. Sew blocks and triangles together in each row. Press seam allowances in opposite directions from row to row.

2. Sew rows together and add small floral setting triangles to each corner of the quilt top. Press the seam toward the setting triangle.

Borders

1. Sew the 1¼"-wide inner border strips together end-to-end in pairs to make 4 long inner border strips.
2. Measure across the center of the quilt from top to bottom. Cut 2 inner border strips to this measurement. Sew a strip to opposite edges of the quilt top. Press the seams toward the borders.
3. Measure across the center of the quilt from side to side including the borders you just added. Cut top and bottom inner borders to this measurement. Sew to the top and bottom edges of the quilt top. Press.
4. Using the 60"-long floral border strips cut earlier, repeat steps 2 and 3 to add the outer borders.

Finishing

1. Layer the quilt top, batting, and backing. Baste the layers together.
2. Mark and quilt as desired or follow the suggestions below. Quilt in the ditch of all seams and use a Baptist fan design in the borders.

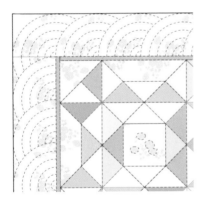

3. Trim the batting and backing even with the quilt top edges.
4. Sew the binding strips together to make one long piece. Bind the edges of the quilt.
5. Add a hanging sleeve if desired. Sign and date your finished quilt.

Home Decorating Hints

A little cupboard, such as this, is a fun place in which to create a small vignette for showing off a special china collection or photographs. Many mail-order catalogs have these cupboards now, or they can be found in antique stores.

Choose florals for a quilt to match a special china set.

Sawtooth Star

*I*FIRST MET MARSHA MCCLOSKEY OVER TWENTY-FIVE YEARS AGO while working my booth at a large craft show. A young woman excitedly approached me carrying a dripping umbrella and towing a reluctant pre-schooler alongside. She had recently moved to Seattle and was thrilled to find a kindred soul. We had many things in common: a passion for quiltmaking; the same wedding anniversary; two children very close in age; and we lived only a mile apart! When I opened my store, Marsha became our first teacher. She taught and sometimes worked on the selling floor, spreading her knowledge and enthusiasm. Marsha started designing a Block of the Month for us in 1980 and went on to bigger things, traveling to teach classes nationally and internationally, writing and publishing books, and designing the popular "Staples" line of fabric for Fabric Sales Company. ∞ Our kids are wonderful adults; the anniversaries have added up; Marsha remains ten years younger; we're still friends—and we haven't lost our passion for quiltmaking. Best of all, Marsha still delivers a pattern every month!

Lovely large cotton chintz florals mix with small cotton prints for a classic decorator look.

Sawtooth Star

Two lovely large-scale floral chintz fabrics combine with smaller-scale fabrics
in this soft quilt. Constructed in bars rather than blocks, the large star blocks
emerge after the top is assembled—but in this scrappy version, you'll have
to look for them. Scraps or fat quarters that complement the floral bouquet
colors are the perfect choice for the sawtooth units.

DESIGNED BY: **Marsha McCloskey**

HAND QUILTED BY: **Virginia Lauth**   FINISHED SIZE: **68¼" x 68¼"**

Tip:

Before you cut the pieces, label 6 small plastic self-sealing bags "Units 1-6." As you cut the pieces for each unit from the designated fabrics, tuck them into the appropriate bag. You will make this quilt in units rather than blocks.

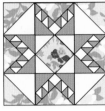

Sawtooth Star

Directions for "Basic Quiltmaking Techniques" begin on page 114.

Cutting Instructions

Cut all strips across the fabric width from selvage to selvage, unless otherwise directed.

Fabric A
- 2 strips, each 2" wide; crosscut 36 squares, each 2" x 2", for Units 2 and 4
- 5 strips, each 2⅜" wide; crosscut 72 squares, each 2⅜" x 2⅜", for Units 2 and 4

Fabric B (assorted greens)
- 54 squares, each 2⅜" x 2⅜", for Units 2 and 4

Fabric B (assorted pinks)
- 54 squares, each 2⅜" x 2⅜", for Units 2 and 4

Fabric C (assorted light prints)
- 18 assorted squares, each 4⅛" x 4⅛"; cut once diagonally for a total of 36 triangles for Unit 1
- 10 squares, each 6¼" x 6¼"; cut once diagonally for 20 triangles for Units 3 and 6
- 16 squares, each 5⅞" x 5⅞", for Unit 5

Fabric D
- 4 lengthwise strips, each 7" x 72", for the outer borders (cut oversize; you will trim later)
- 1 strip 5" x 72" wide; crosscut 9 squares, each 5" x 5", for Unit 1
- 2 strips, each 4⅛" x 72"; crosscut 34 squares, each 4⅛" x 4⅛"; cut once diagonally for 70 triangles for Units 2 and 4 (cut two more squares from 5"-wide strips for 4 more triangles)

Fabric E
- 1 strip, 7⅝" wide; crosscut 3 squares, 7⅝" x 7⅝"; cut twice diagonally for a total of 12 triangles for Unit 2
- 2 strips, each 5¼" wide; crosscut 12 squares, each 5¼" x 5¼", for Unit 4
- 1 strip, 8" wide; crosscut 4 squares, each 8" x 8", for Unit 6
- 3 strips, each 5⅞" wide; crosscut 8 rectangles, each 5⅞" x 11¼", for Unit 5

From the remainder of the 7⅝"-wide strip
- 2 squares, each 6¼" x 6¼"; cut once diagonally for a total of 4 triangles for Unit 3

Inner Border
- 7 strips, each 2" wide

Binding
- 7 strips, each 2½" wide

Units One and Six Assembly

1. Sew a 4⅛" light (Fabric C) triangle to opposite sides of each 5" dark Floral Bouquet (Fabric D) square. Press the seams toward the triangles. Add two more triangles to each square in the same manner. Press.

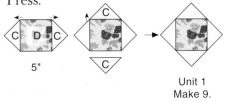

Unit 1
Make 9.

Sawtooth Star

**Fabric Requirements
44"-wide fabrics**

- Light fabric for Sawtooth units (Fabric A) - ⅝ yd.
- Assorted pink prints and green prints for Sawtooth units (Fabric B) - ¾ yd. total
- Assorted prints on light background (Fabric C) - 1½ yds. total
- Large Floral Bouquet on dark green ground for blocks and outer borders (Fabric D) - 2½ yds.
- Large Floral Bouquet on medium-green ground for blocks (Fabric E) - 1½ yds.
- Pink print for inner border - ½ yd.
- Pink print for binding - ⅝ yd.
- Backing - 4¼ yds.
- Batting - 75" x 75" piece

2. Repeat step 1, using 8" medium floral bouquet (Fabric E) squares and 6¼" light (Fabric C) triangles.

Note: For a scrappy look, prints need not match around large squares.

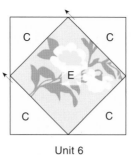

Unit 6
Make 4.

Unit Three Assembly

1. With right sides together and raw edges even, position each 6¼" light print (Fabric C) triangle on a 6¼" medium background floral bouquet (Fabric E) triangle.
2. Stitch. Press the seams toward the darker triangle. Make 4.

Unit 3 (corners)
Make 4.

Unit Five Assembly

1. Draw a diagonal line on the wrong side of the 5⅞" light print (Fabric C) squares.

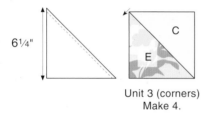

Fabric C
Mark 16.

2. Position a square at one corner of each medium floral bouquet 5⅞" x 11¼" (Fabric E) rectangle as shown and stitch on the drawn line. Trim the corner ¼" from the stitching and press the seam toward the triangle.

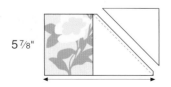

11¼"

3. Position a square at the opposite corner of each unit. Stitch, trim, and press.

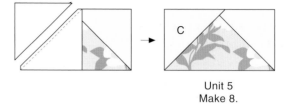

Unit 5
Make 8.

Units Two and Four Assembly

1. To make half-square triangle units: Draw a diagonal line on the wrong side of each 2⅜" light (Fabric A) square. Position each light square on a 2⅜" pink or green print square (Fabric B) with right sides together. Stitch ¼" from the line on each side. Cut on the line. Press toward dark triangle

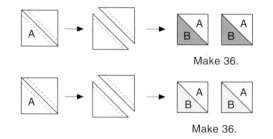

Make 36.

Make 36.

2. Cut the remaining 2⅜" pink (18) and green (18) squares (Fabric B) in half once diagonally for a total of 72 triangles.

2⅜"

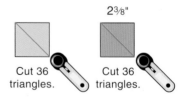

Cut 36 triangles.   Cut 36 triangles.

3. Arrange the half-square triangle units from step 1 with the 2" light squares (Fabric A) and the pink and green triangles from step 2 to make the required number of Units A and B. Press seams in the direction of the arrows.

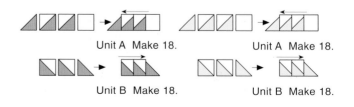

Unit A Make 18.   Unit A Make 18.

Unit B Make 18.   Unit B Make 18.

4. Using Units A and B from step 3, and the triangles of the dark-background floral (Fabric D), and squares and triangles of the medium-background floral (Fabric E), assemble Units Two and Four. Follow the piecing diagrams below and press seams in the direction of the arrows.

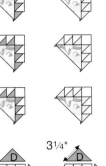

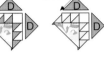

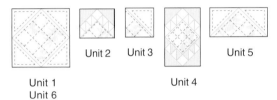

3¼"

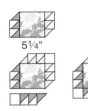

5¼"

Unit 2
Make 6.

Unit 2
Make 6.

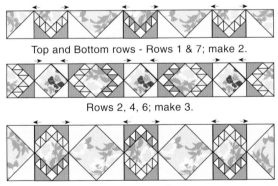

Unit 4
Make 12.

Quilt Top Assembly

1. Following the diagram, arrange and sew the units together in rows. Press seams in the direction of the arrows.

Top and Bottom rows - Rows 1 & 7; make 2.

Rows 2, 4, 6; make 3.

Rows 3 & 5; make 2.

2. Sew the rows together in numerical order, matching seams carefully. Be sure to place the top and bottom rows correctly so the long edge of the large triangle is at the top and bottom edges of the quilt top. Press seams in one direction.

Borders

1. Measure the quilt top length through the center and trim 2 border strips to this measurement. Sew to the long edges of the quilt top. Press the seams toward the border.
2. Measure the quilt top width through the center, including the border strips you just added, and cut remaining 2 border strips to this measurement. Sew to the top and bottom edges of the quilt top. Press the seams toward the borders.
3. Repeat steps 1 and 2 to add outer borders to the quilt top.

Finishing

1. Layer the quilt top, batting, and backing. Baste the layers together.
2. Mark and quilt as desired or follow the quilting suggestion below.

Unit 1
Unit 6

Unit 2 Unit 3

Unit 4

Unit 5

3. Trim the batting and backing even with the quilt top edges.
4. Sew the binding strips together to make one long piece. Bind the edges of the quilt.
5. Add a hanging sleeve if desired. Sign and date your finished quilt.

Home Decorating Hints

Match your wall colors to a quilt. It's usually wise to choose a paint color several tints lighter and grayer than the color in the quilt. Buy the smallest amount of paint available to paint a large test square. Notice the color at different times of the day, with lamps on and off.

Seaside Garden

TRISH MADE THIS QUILT TO REMIND HER OF THE MANY HAPPY days she has spent on the East Coast at the beach. She wanted to mix large florals and plaids to achieve a whimsical, summer-cottage look. ∞ We had so much fun collecting knickknacks and accessories for the photo sessions for this book, but we were always nervous about the setup.

One day we went to Seattle's famous Pike Place Market for flowers and found the lovely sweet peas we visualized for this photo. The vases containing the flowers were perfect coordinating colors for Trish's Seaside Garden quilt, but they were not for sale! ∞ We used our best bargaining techniques, and the young woman, who spoke little English, relented. "Okay—twenty dollar," she said. We thanked her, gave her the money and walked away beaming. ∞ As we were setting up for the photography, we noticed the initials "K.C." inked on each vase in letters an inch high. We laughed and decided it must be a message to "Keep Clam"—a laid-back Seattle expression. We turned the vases around and serenely readied the scene for the photo shoot.

Summertime cotton and linen blend florals combine with cotton prints for a pretty textured wall hanging.

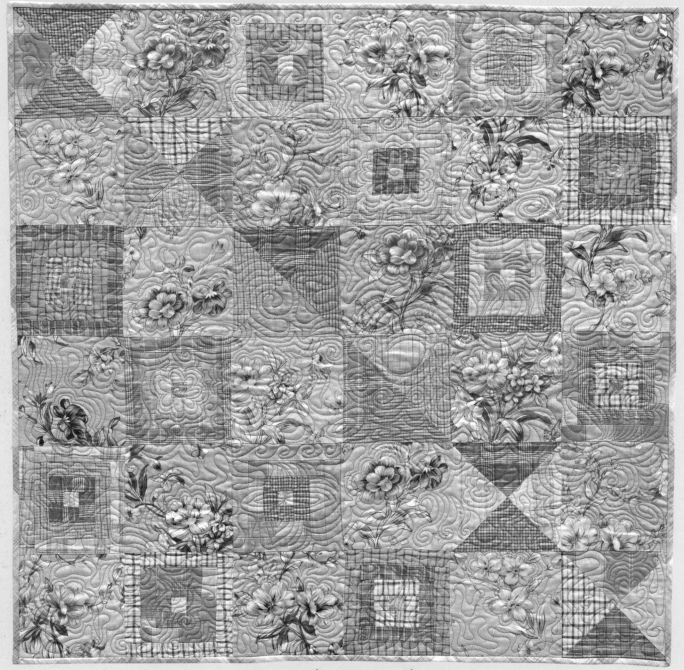

Seaside Garden

Pair your favorite florals with softly coordinating plaids and stripes to make this quick-and-easy lap quilt or wall hanging. It's easy to upsize this one—just make more Plaid Log Cabin and Scrappy Hourglass blocks and cut more squares of your floral fabrics. With no borders to add, this lively quilt is easy to make in a day!

DESIGNED BY: **Trish Carey**   QUILTED BY: **Maradie Birmingham**

FINISHED SIZE: **37½" x 37½"**   FINISHED BLOCK SIZE: **6¼" x 6¼"**

Scrappy
Strips

Scrappy
Hourglass

Floral
Onepatch

Directions for "Basic Quiltmaking Techniques" begin on page 114.

Cutting Instructions

Floral Bouquet
- 18 squares total, each 6¾" x 6¾" (4 squares *each* of pink and green) (5 squares *each* of yellow and blue)

Tone-on-tone prints
- 12 squares, each 1½" x 1½" (3 each of four colors)

Assorted plaids
- 1 square, 7½" x 7½", from each plaid; cut twice diagonally for 4 triangles; you will need only 2 of each color for the blocks (24 total). See "Plaid Cabin Block Assembly" at right for additional cutting directions.

Plaid for Binding
- 2½"-wide bias strips to total 5½ yds.

Hourglass Block Assembly

All seam allowances are ¼" wide.

1. Arrange the triangles in scrappy sets of four.

2. Sew triangles together in pairs and press all seams in the same direction.

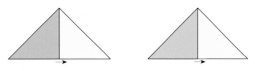

3. Sew the triangle pairs together to complete each block. Press.

Scrappy Hourglass
Make 6.
Assorted color combinations

Plaid Cabin Block Assembly

1. Choose three different plaids and one 1½" tone-on-tone square for the first block.
2. Cut a 1⅜"-wide strip from each plaid fabric.
3. With right sides together, stitch the square to a plaid strip. Trim the strip edges even with the square and press the seam away from the center square.

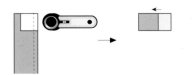

Seaside Garden

Fabric Requirements
44"-wide fabric

Note: Fat quarters are 18" x 20-22" pieces; fat eights are 9" x 20-22" pieces.
- Floral Bouquet fabrics - ¼ yd *each*, yellow and blue; 1 fat quarter *each*, medium scale pink and green
- Tone-on-tone prints (pink, green, yellow, blue) - scraps for Plaid Cabin block centers
- 12 different plaids (pink, green, yellow, blue) - fat eighths for Plaid Cabin and Hourglass blocks
- Backing - 1¼ yds. of a single fabric, or piece several fabrics together to make a 42" square
- Batting - 42" x 42" piece
- Binding - ½ yd. plaid for bias-cut binding

4. With right sides together, sew a strip of the same plaid to the twopatch piece from step 3. Trim the strip even with the twopatch edges and press the seam away from the twopatch.

5. Working clockwise around the piece, add two more strips of the same plaid to the block, cutting additional 1⅜"-wide strips as needed. Trim and press away from the center after each addition.

6. Always working around the block in a clockwise direction and pressing away from the center, add four strips of each of the two remaining plaids to the block. Make a total of 12 Log Cabin blocks, using the remaining center squares and plaid fabrics.

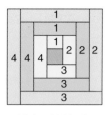

Make 12 blocks
in assorted color
combinations.

Quilt Top Assembly

1. Arrange the blocks in 6 rows of 6 blocks each, following the quilt diagram for placement. Note how the color placement of the floral squares runs in diagonal rows in one direction and alternates on the diagonal in the opposite direction.

2. Sew the blocks together in rows, and press the seams in opposite directions from row to row.

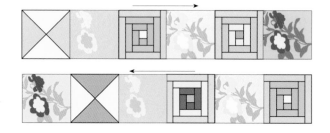

3. To complete the quilt top, sew the rows together, taking care to match seam intersections. Press seams in one direction.

Finishing

1. Layer the quilt with batting and backing.
2. Baste the quilt layers together. Mark and quilt as desired. The quilt shown was quilted in meandering curves across the entire surface.

3. Trim the excess batting and backing even with the quilt top edges.
4. Sew the bias strips for the binding together to create one long strip. Bind the quilt edges.
5. Add a hanging sleeve if desired. Sign and date your quilt.

Home Decorating Hints

— Make one wall in a small room an accent for your quilted wall hanging by shirring coordinating fabric on rods. This may cover the entire wall or only a small portion of the wall around the quilt. We also basted a lace valance flat against the rod.

— Show shell collections in jars or display them freestanding as decorative objects. These are great collections for kids.

Seattle Stars

I NAMED THIS QUILT AS A TONGUE-IN-CHEEK REFERENCE TO THE many starless nights we have in Seattle. You have to look very closely to find the stars in the quilt as the positioning of the light, medium, and dark fabrics make the stars disappear. ❧ In our store we sell a kit for this quilt. A customer saw the quilt advertised in our newsletter and

called to request we send it along with some other tempting fabrics. We filled the order and sent it downstairs for packaging. ❧ We buy recycled shipping boxes that are mostly over-runs from other companies so the lettering on the boxes is always a surprise. The order was packaged and the box sent out and delivered to the doorstep of the customer who had left a note saying, "U.P.S., Please deliver any packages to my neighbor at…" The neighbor accepted the box and when she saw the "Seattle Salmon" lettering, immediately put it in her freezer. ❧ When our customer returned home and retrieved her package, she called us to say she was thrilled with her "cool stuff."

Two floral bouquet fabrics, one light and one dark, blend to create a romantic wall quilt or throw.

Seattle Stars

Designed so the stars aren't easily recognized, this quilt is an irreverent tribute to the cloudy evenings in Seattle. But the stars do shine and flowers do bloom in Seattle—even in the rain! Carefully planned Hourglass blocks create the shaded effect in the sashing that surround large Onepatch floral bouquets, just as the gray skies often shroud Seattle in the mist.

DESIGNED BY: **Sharon Yenter**   QUILTED BY: **Laurie Shifrin**

FINISHED SIZE: **57½" x 57½"**   FINISHED BLOCK SIZE: **Floral Bouquet Onepatch 8" x 8"**

Hourglass Sashing Squares 4" x 4"

Floral Bouquet
Onepatch

Hourglass

Directions for "Basic Quiltmaking Techniques" begin on page 114.

Cutting Instructions

Cut strips across the width of the fabric from selvage to selvage, unless otherwise directed.

Floral Bouquet #1 (light background)

- 3 strips, each 8½" wide; crosscut 9 squares, each 8½" x 8½"
- 2 strips, each 4½" wide; crosscut 16 squares, each 4½" x 4½"

Floral Bouquet #2 (blue background)

- 4 lengthwise strips, each 7½" wide; cut each entire strip from length of fabric—you will trim to size later; cut selectively to place the same section of the floral pattern in each border.

Light blue tone-on-tone print

- 2 strips, each 5¼" wide; crosscut 12 squares, each 5¼" x 5¼"

Medium blue print

- 4 strips, each 5¼" wide; crosscut 24 squares, each 5¼" x 5¼"

Dark blue tone-on-tone print

- 2 strips, each 5¼" wide; crosscut 12 squares, each 5¼" x 5¼"

Red plaid

- 6 lengthwise strips, each 1¾" wide; you will trim to size later

Binding

- 7 strips, each 2½" wide

Seattle Stars

Fabric Requirements
44"-wide fabrics

- Floral Bouquet #1 (light background) for blocks and sashing squares - 1⅛ yd.
- Floral Bouquet #2 (blue background) for outer border - 2⅛ yds.
- Light blue tone-on-tone print for sashing blocks - ⅜ yd.
- Medium blue print for sashing blocks - ¾ yd.
- Dark blue tone-on-tone print for sashing blocks - ⅜ yd.
- Red plaid for inner border - 1½ yds.
- Binding - ⅝ yd.
- Backing - 3⅝ yds.
- Batting - 62" x 62" piece

Sashing Block Assembly

1. Using a pencil and ruler, draw diagonal lines from corner to corner on the wrong side of each 5¼" medium blue square. Place a marked square face down on each light blue and dark blue square. On each pair of squares, stitch ¼" from both sides of one marked line.

2. Cut the squares on both drawn lines to yield 48 light and 48 dark pieced triangles. Press all seams toward the medium blue triangle in each one.

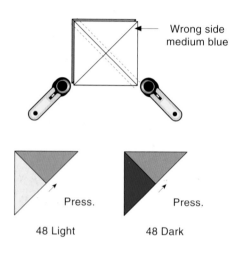

3. Stitch each light pieced triangle to a dark pieced triangle, matching seam intersections carefully. Press the seams in one direction. Make 48 pieced sashing squares.

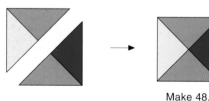

Make 48.

4. Stitch two pieced squares together with the dark blue triangles together. Make 24.

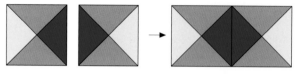

Make 24.

Quilt Top Assembly

1. Arrange 3 pieced sashing rectangles with the 4½" floral bouquet squares to create a sashing row. Press the seams toward the floral bouquet squares. Make 4 rows.

Sashing Row
Make 4.

2. Arrange 4 pieced sashing rectangles with 8½" floral bouquet Onepatch blocks to make a block row. Press the seams toward the floral bouquet blocks. Make 3.

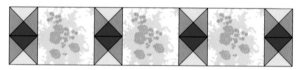

Block Row
Make 3.

3. Referring to the photo of the quilt on page 110, arrange the block and sashing rows in alternating fashion, beginning and ending with a sashing row. Sew the rows together and press the seams in one direction.

Borders

1. Trim the plaid border strips to 46" long and sew to the quilt top, following directions for mitered borders on pages 117 and 118. Press the seams toward the plaid borders.
2. Measure the quilt top length through the center, including the plaid borders. Trim 2 Floral Bouquet #2 7½"-wide border strips to this measurement. Sew to opposite edges of the quilt top. Press seams toward the plaid borders.
3. Measure the quilt top width through the center, including the borders you just added. Trim the remaining 2 floral borders to this measurement and sew to the top and bottom edges of the quilt top. Press the seams toward the plaid borders.

Finishing

1. Layer the quilt top, batting, and backing. Baste the layers together.
2. Mark and quilt as desired. In the quilt shown, all seams were quilted in the ditch and quilting was done around selected floral motifs in each floral block. You can do the same in the border or use a favorite all-over pattern such as Baptist fan or Clamshell.
3. Trim the batting and backing even with the quilt top edges.
4. Sew the binding strips together to make one long piece. Bind the edges of the quilt.
5. Add a hanging sleeve if desired. Sign and date your finished quilt.

Home Decorating Hints

↝ Use this size quilt for a sofa throw or TV quilt.

↝ Use a library table behind your sofa to display flowers and a collection that coordinates with the quilt. This adds color to your room and is an inexpensive way to generate warmth and charm.

Basic Quiltmaking Techniques

The basic techniques you will need to know to make and finish the quilts in this book are included on the following pages.

Rotary Cutting Basics

With a few exceptions, you can cut the pieces for any of the quilts in this book using a rotary cutter, ruler, and mat. If you don't already own rotary cutting tools, choose a cutter that fits comfortably in your hand, a self-healing mat, and an acrylic ruler that measures at least 6" x 18" and is marked with measurements in ¼" and ⅛" increments. If you have never done any rotary cutting, practice on scrap fabric first. The blade is very sharp so it's not necessary to press too hard when you first begin—but be sure to place even pressure on the blade as you cut. *Always remember to close the blade each time you finish cutting.* The rotary cutter can be a dangerous tool if not used with proper care.

Cutting Strips

1. Fold the fabric in half lengthwise with selvages together. Fold again if desired, and position it on the cutting mat.
2. Align the top edge of the ruler (or one of the horizontal marks) with the upper folded edge and cover the raw edges of the fabric. Make the first cut to trim away the excess and create a straight edge that is perpendicular to the folded edge. While holding the ruler firmly in place, position the blade of the cutter alongside the ruler at the end closest to you. Bear down and move the cutter away from you, cutting through all layers. "Walk" the hand along the ruler to maintain pressure next to the cutter as it cuts. Discard the cutaway.

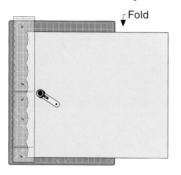

3. To cut strips, refer to the quilt directions for the correct strip width. Locate that measurement on the right-hand edge of the ruler (reverse position if you are left-handed) and place the line over the clean-cut, straight edge of the folded fabric. Make sure that a horizontal line on the ruler lines up with the top or bottom fold of the fabric so the strip will be straight. If you cannot line up the cutting measurement and a horizontal line, repeat steps 1 and 2 to get a straight cut on the edge. Cut the strip, beginning at the fabric fold closest to you and cutting to the opposite edge of the fabric. Be sure to hold the ruler firmly in place.

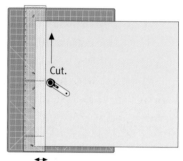

Strip Width

Cutting Shapes

The quilts in this book require simple shapes—squares, rectangles, and triangles. Unless you are directed to selectively cut pieces for the quilt you are making, you will first cut strips and then cut the strips into the required shapes. (For selective cutting, see page 21).

Squares and Rectangles

1. Cut a strip of the required width (see your quilt pattern directions).
2. Carefully turn the strip parallel to the length of your cutting mat and align one cut edge with a horizontal line. Position the ruler with the appropriate line for the desired square or rectangle size along the short end of the strip. Cut through all layers.

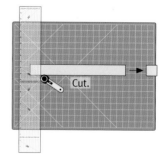

Triangles

To cut triangles, first cut strips, then cut into squares of the size specified in the directions.

1. To cut half-square triangles, cut a square in half on the diagonal. The diagonal edges of resulting triangles are on the bias, with the short sides of the triangle on the straight of grain.

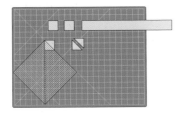

To allow for seam allowances, the strips and squares are cut $\frac{7}{8}$" larger than the finished size.

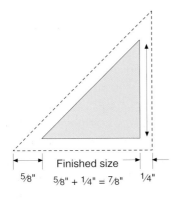

Finished size
$\frac{5}{8}$" $\frac{5}{8}$" + $\frac{1}{4}$" = $\frac{7}{8}$" $\frac{1}{4}$"

2. To cut quarter-square triangles, first cut a square in half on the diagonal. Without moving the cut pieces, reposition the ruler on the remaining diagonal and cut again for 4 quarter-square triangles. Quarter-square triangles are required for the side setting triangles in many of the quilts shown in this book.

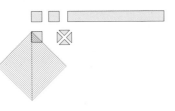

The diagonal edge of each of these triangles is on the straight of grain so that when the block or quilt is assembled this edge will not stretch. To allow for seam allowances, the strips and squares are cut $1\frac{1}{4}$" larger than the finished size.

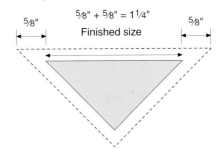

$\frac{5}{8}$" $\frac{5}{8}$" + $\frac{5}{8}$" = $1\frac{1}{4}$" $\frac{5}{8}$"
Finished size

General Piecing Directions

Ideally, if pieces are cut and sewn precisely, patchwork designs will come out flat and smooth with crisply matched corners and points. In practice, it doesn't always happen that way. Here are four matching techniques that can be helpful in many different piecing situations.

1. **Opposing seams.** When stitching one seamed unit to another, press seam allowances on the seams that need to match in opposite directions. The two "opposing" seams will hold each other in place and evenly distribute the bulk. Plan pressing to take advantage of opposing seams.

2. **Positioning pin.** Carefully push a pin straight through two points that must be matched and pull the two pieces tightly together. With the positioning pin in place, pin the seam as you normally would and then remove the positioning pin.

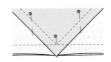

3. **The X.** When triangles are pieced, stitches form an X at the next seam line. Stitch through the center of the X to avoid chopping off the points on the sewn triangles.

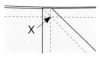

4. **Easing.** When two pieces to be sewn together must match but instead are slightly different lengths, pin the points of matching and stitch with the shorter piece on top. The feed dogs will ease in the fullness of the bottom piece as you stitch.

It is possible to piece beautifully and accurately with a sewing machine. Try to correct mistakes when they happen—keep a seam ripper handy—but don't spend too much time ripping out and restitching. Some sewing inaccuracies can be corrected; others cannot. Sometimes the best thing is to move on and make the next block better. The quality of your piecing will improve with each block you piece.

Piecing the Blocks

Accurate stitching is essential to good quilt-making. All the quilts in this book were planned and made with ¼"-wide seam allowances. If you do not have a ¼"-quilter's presser foot for your machine, it is very important to mark an accurate ¼" seamline on your machine. To do so:

1. Cut a 2" x 4" piece of ¼" graph paper, cutting accurately along the lines.
2. Position the graph paper under the presser foot and carefully lower the needle into the first line from the right-hand edge of the paper. Lower the foot to anchor the paper and make sure that the edge is straight and perpendicular to the needle position.

3. Place a piece of masking tape or a ¼" x 1" strip of Dr. Scholl's moleskin on the sewing machine with the edge aligned with the edge of the paper. If you are using masking tape, use several layers to build up a "ledge" against which to guide the raw edges of each seam as you stitch.

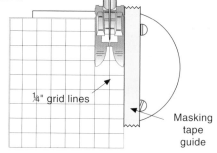

¼" grid lines

Masking tape guide

Chain Piecing

Use chain piecing whenever possible to speed up your sewing and save thread.

1. Sew the first set of pieces together and continue stitching off the edge for a few stitches, creating a "chain" of thread.
2. Without lifting the presser foot, arrange the next set of pieces and feed it under the foot while you stitch. Continue in this manner until you have finished stitching the first set of seams in the block you are making.
3. At the ironing board, clip the threads between the stitched units.
4. Press the seams following the pressing directions for the block you are making. Usually seams are pressed toward the darker patch in a unit, but sometimes it is necessary to press a seam toward the lighter piece in a particular block to make it easier to match up the seamlines in the next step. To avoid distorted blocks, avoid stretching the pieces as you press.

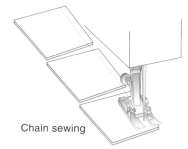

Chain sewing

Adding Borders

The borders for most of the quilts in this book were cut and attached to the sides and then to the top and bottom edges of the quilt top. These are called straight-cut borders. A few borders have mitered corners. If you prefer mitered corners, you may need additional yardage to cut the border strips. Measuring accurately to determine the cut lengths for either type of border is essential to ensure a flat quilt without rippled edges.

Attaching Straight-Cut Borders

1. Measure the quilt top length through the center and cut two side borders to match this measurement. On large quilts, it's a good idea to measure the length along both outer edges as well and use an average of the three measurements to cut the border strips.

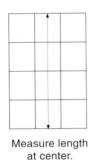

Measure length
at center.

2. Mark the quilt top center and quarter points and do the same on each long border.
3. Pin the border to the quilt top with centers and quarter points matching and raw edges even at each end.
4. Stitch the border to the quilt top, slightly easing or stretching the quilt top as needed for a perfect fit. Press the seam allowance as instructed in the directions for the quilt you are making.

5. Repeat steps 1-4 to measure the quilt width, including the borders you just added, cut, and attach the top and bottom borders.

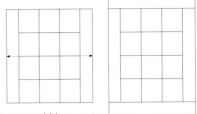

Measure width at center
after adding side borders.

Attaching Borders with Mitered Corners

1. Estimate the finished outer dimensions of the quilt top after the borders have been added. For example, if your quilt top is 45" x 65" and the finished border width is 8", the quilt top will measure 61" x 81" (quilt dimensions plus two finished border widths). Cut border strips to these dimensions plus at least 2" extra for seam allowances and adjustments. It's always a good idea to play it safe and cut the strips a little longer than necessary.
2. Measure the quilt top through the center in both directions and note the measurements.
3. Mark the centers and quarter points on all four edges of the quilt top.
4. With pins, mark the length of the quilt top on the side border strips. Also mark the center and quarter points.

Length of quilt at center

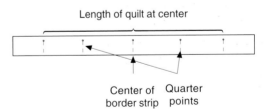

Center of   Quarter
border strip   points

5. Pin the side borders to the quilt top, matching raw edges at the outer pins, centers, and quarter points.

6. Stitch, beginning and ending the stitching ¼" from the raw edges of the quilt top.

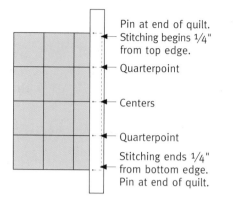

Pin at end of quilt.
Stitching begins 1/4"
from top edge.

Quarterpoint

Centers

Quarterpoint

Stitching ends 1/4"
from bottom edge.
Pin at end of quilt.

7. Repeat with the top and bottom borders.

8. Working on a large, flat, padded surface or the ironing board, fold the quilt so that the borders at one corner of the quilt are aligned with right sides together and raw edges even. Pin the borders together as shown. If possible, anchor the quilt top to the work surface with pins. Use a ruler and pencil to draw a 45° stitching line on the wrong side of the border. Begin at the end of the stitching and keep the edge of the ruler even with the folded edge of the quilt top.

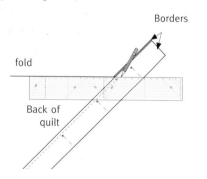

Borders

fold

Back of
quilt

9. Machine baste on the drawn line. Open out the corner and check for accuracy. Adjust if necessary.

10. Stitch on the drawn line, beginning at the inner corner and ending at the border raw edges. Trim the excess, leaving a ¼"-wide seam allowance.

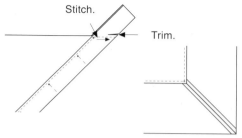

Stitch.

Trim.

11. Press the seam open. Repeat with the remaining three corners.

Quilt Finishing

Prepare the backing. For quilts that measure larger than 38" wide, you will need to piece the backing by cutting and sewing two or more lengths of fabric together.

1. Measure the completed quilt top and add 4" to each dimension for a working allowance. For example, if your finished quilt top measures 45" x 56", you will need a backing that measures at least 49" x 60".

2. To create a backing of the required width, cut the required lengths and sew together. Press the seam(s) open. You can sew two lengths together or you can split the second length and sew the pieces to the opposite sides of one backing piece. Sometimes, it's best to cut and piece the backing so the seams are across the width of the quilt top, to eliminate fabric waste.

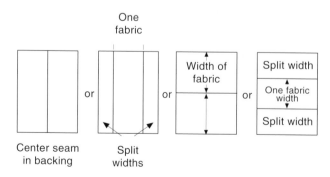

One
fabric

or

or

Width of
fabric

or

Split width

One fabric
width

Split width

Center seam
in backing

Split
widths

3. Cut a piece of batting the same size as the backing.

Layering the Quilt

1. Place the backing, face down, on a large, flat surface and smooth it out so there are no wrinkles. Clamp to a table with bull-nose clips, or use masking tape to hold it in place. The backing should be flat and slightly taut but not stretched off grain.
2. Center the batting on top of the backing, taking care not to stretch or distort it. Pat into place, eliminating wrinkles.
3. Press the completed quilt top and center on top of the batting.
4. Use safety pins to hold the layers together, spacing them no more than a hand's width apart, or hand baste through all layers in the pattern shown, using light-colored thread (dark colors may bleed onto your quilt top when you remove them).

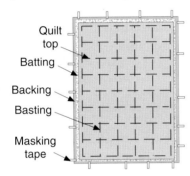

5. Hand or machine quilt as desired through all layers, using your choice of designs or following the suggestions that accompany each quilt in this book.

Binding the Quilt

Most of the quilts in this book were finished with a double-layer binding cut along the straight grain. Some were finished with double-layer bias strips. In either case, the strips are cut 2½" wide and must be sewn together to create a continuous piece of binding.

1. After completing the quilting, trim the batting and backing even with the raw edges of the quilt top, making sure that edges are straight, the borders are an even width, and the corners are square.
2. Using diagonal seams, sew the binding strips together as shown. Trim excess, leaving a ¼"-wide seam allowance. Press the seams open.

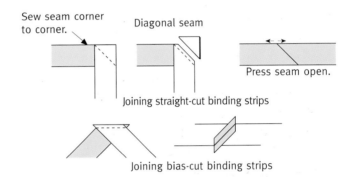

3. Fold the binding in half lengthwise with wrong sides together and press, taking care not to stretch it. At one end, open out the fold and turn the raw edge in at a 45° angle. Press. Trim, leaving a ¼" allowance.

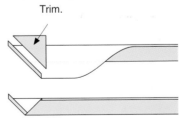

4. Beginning on one edge of the quilt a few inches from a corner, pin the binding to the quilt top. Beginning two inches from the folded end of the binding, stitch ⅜" from the raw edges and stop ⅜" from the raw edge at the corner. Backstitch and remove the quilt.

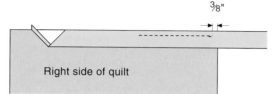

5. Fold the binding back on itself to create a 45° angle, then turn the binding down to make a fold in the binding that is in line with the upper raw edge of the quilt top. Pin. Stitch the binding to the quilt, ending ⅜" from the next corner. Backstitch and miter the corner as you did the previous one.

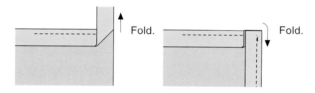

6. Continue in this manner until the binding has been stitched to all four edges of the quilt top. When you reach the beginning of the binding, trim away excess, leaving 1" to tuck into the folded binding. Complete the stitching.

7. Turn the binding to the back of the quilt and hand sew in place, mitering corners as shown.

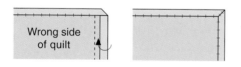

The Final Touches

If you plan to use your completed quilt as a wall hanging, you will need to add a hanging sleeve to the back. You can do it after the quilt is completed but it's faster, easier, and sturdier if you catch it in the seam when you attach the binding to the top edge of the quilt.

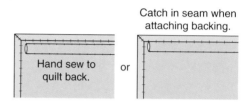

1. Cut a strip of fabric the length of your quilt top and 8"-10" wide.

2. Turn under and press ½" at each short end. Then turn and press each hem again and stitch.

3. With wrong sides together, fold the strip in half lengthwise and press.

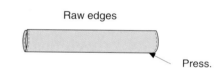

4. Machine baste the sleeve to the quilt with raw edges even, centering it on the back of the quilt.

Baste sleeve to upper edge of quilt.

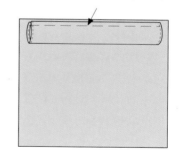

5. Apply the binding following the directions on page 119.
6. Slipstitch the long edge of the sleeve in place through the backing only, allowing a little slack as shown so the sleeve will take some of the weight of the quilt and the shape of the hanging rod when hung.

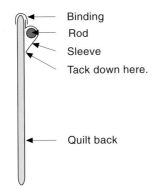

Binding

Rod

Sleeve

Tack down here.

Quilt back

7. Hand sew the short ends of the underlayer of the sleeve to the quilt.

Add a label to your quilt to document who made it, when, and where, plus any other information you would like to add for posterity's sake.

A quilt label can be as simple or as elaborate as you wish. For a simple label, just write the information on a scrap of muslin with an indelible pen. Apply the shiny side of a piece of freezer paper to the wrong side of the fabric before you write to stabilize the fabric, then remove the paper before sewing the label to the back of the quilt.

Acknowledgements

In The Beginning has always been a team effort. I have been blessed by being surrounded with capable, enthusiastic, and fun people. Every successful business person knows that if you surround yourself with talented people, encourage and allow their creativity, they will make you look good.

With much thanks and appreciation...

To my husband, Bill, who tolerates my bouts of obsessive creativity, stands back and lets me go!

To my son and business partner (read boss), Jason, who makes working at In The Beginning a joy.

To Jason's wife, Kristi, the daughter we never had, who makes me proud every day.

To my son, Ben, who has encouraged me since he was a baby, smiling and chattering while I sewed and sewed and sewed!

To my Mom, Florence, who has always been a big part of In The Beginning and has more talent than Martha Stewart!

To our hardworking and knowledgeable In The Beginning staff, who have made the store and Wholesale Division a success. We are so lucky to have you all with us.

To the staff at Sea-Hill Press, who can work magic and bring ideas to life. Greg, Barbara S., Laura, Barbara W., Heather, Brian, Wendy, Jamie, it was a delight working with you— you're the best!

To Ken, our favorite photographer, who always brings humor and expertise to any project.

Special thanks to Trish, Margy, Laurie, Maradie, Sherry Rogers of Runway Ranch Quilting, Jackie Quinn, Marsha McCloskey, Julie Sheckman, David Peha of Fabric Sales, Inc., the people at Northcott Silk, Inc., and especially Paul O'Rourke and Bernie Berlin who offered me the opportunity of a lifetime.

Credits

Produced by: Sea-Hill Press, Inc.

6101 200th St. SW, Suite 205

Lynnwood, WA 98036

Telephone 425.697.3606

President: Greg Sharp

Technical Writer: Barbara Weiland

Editor: Laura M. Reinstatler

Copy Editor: Wendy Slotboom

Photography: Ken Wagner

Photo Styling: Sharon Yenter, Trish Carey, Jason Yenter

Cover and Text Design: Barbara Schmitt

Illustrations: Brian Metz

Graphic Assistant: Heather Bauerle

Assistant: Jamie Trubia

Floral Bouquet Quilts From In The Beginning
© 2001 Sharon Evans Yenter
In The Beginning, Seattle, Washington USA

ISBN 1-9706900-0-3

Printed in Hong Kong

In The Beginning staff members who contributed to this book,
from left to right: Sharon Yenter, Jason Yenter, Trish Carey,
Laurie Shifrin, Margy Duncan.

Recommended Books

Color & Quiltmaking:

Color Harmony Workbook, Rockport Publishers, Glouchester, MA, 1999

Color Magic for Quilters, Emmaus, Seely, Ann and Stewart, Joyce, PA, Rodale Press, Inc., 1997

Color – The Quilters Guide, Barnes, Christine, Seattle, WA, That Patchwork Place, 1997

Express Yourself With Color, Better Homes and Gardens Books, Des Moines, IA, Meredith Corp., 1998

Color In the American Home, Wills, Margaret Sabo, Upper Saddle River, NJ, Creative Homeowner, 1998

Design Essentials, Torrance, Lorraine, Seattle, WA, That Patchwork Place, 1998

Machine Quilting, Noble, Maurine, Seattle, WA, That Patchwork Place, 1999

Home Decorating:

Country Living's Country Quilts, Sears, Mary Seehafer, New York, William Morrow & Co., Inc., 1992

Cottage Style, Better Homes and Gardens Books, Des Moines, IA, Meredith Corp., 1998

Shabby Chic, Ashwell, Rachael, New York, Harper Collins Publishers, Inc., 1996

Rachael Ashwell's Shabby Chic, Ashwell, Rachael, New York, Harper Collins Publishers, Inc., 1998

The Shabby Chic Home, Ashwell, Rachael, New York, Harper Collins Publishers, Inc., 1999

Guide to Pattern & Color, Creative Publishing International, Minnetonka, MN, Creative Publishing International, 1998

Women and History:

Anonymous Was a Woman, Bank, Mirra, New York, St. Martins Press, 1979

We Are Our Mothers' Daughters, Roberts, Cokie, New York, William Morrow and Co., Inc. 1998

Quilts, The Great American Art, Mainardi, Patricia, San Pedro, CA, Miles & Weir, LTD., 1978

The Quilters, Women and Domestic Art, Cooper, Patricia and Buferd, Norma Bradley, New York, Doubleday & Co., Inc., 1977

Quilts in America, Orlofsky, Patsy & Myron, New York, Reprint edition, Abbeville Press, 1992

Glorious American Quilts, Warren, Elizabeth V., and Eisenstat, Sharon L., New York, Penguin Studios, 1996

Clues in the Calico, Brackman, Barbara, Washington D.C., EPM Publications, 1989

Quilt Treasures of Great Britain, The Quilters Guild, Nashville, TN, Rutledge Hill Press, 1995

Simple Abundance, A Daybook of Comfort and Joy, Breathnach, Sarah Ban, New York, Warner Books, Inc., 1995

Resources

Many of the fabrics featured in this book are available at your local quilt shop or you may inquire at:
    In The Beginning Fabrics
    8201 Lake City Way NE
    Seattle, Washington 98115
    206.523.8862
    www.inthebeginningfabrics.com